CONSCIOUSNESS
& The WORLD

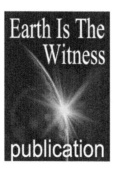

Earth Is The
Witness

publication

CONSCIOUSNESS & The WORLD

Narrations of AWAKENING

UNIVERSAL WISDOM FOR SPIRITUAL ENLIGHTENMENT

Petar Umiljanovic

DISCLAIMER

Thank You for Your Contribution !

Cover design by
Petar Umiljanovic

Earth Is The Witness

This is my Intellect
my Heart & Soul

speaking to You
in words of
Infinite Consciousness

my endless Love
for this World

for You

As You read it through

it will reward You
being forever written in
the Universe's Book of Life

I LOVE YOU

THE

JOURNEY

1. *BEGINNING*

2. *UNIVERSE*

3. HUMAN

4. ILLUSION

5. TRAVELLING

6. LETTING GO

7. AWAKENING

8. NATURE

9. CONSCIOUSNESS

10. THE WORLD

Thank You !

INTRODUCTION

WELCOME, DEAR READER !

Philosophy means the Love of Wisdom, and it indicates
Human, or any other Conscious need to Know and Understand
all the inner workings of Life, of Nature, and the Universe.

In This Book, We're going to honour that inquisition as We look at the
Fundamental Nature of Reality, Consciousness, and its many implications
for The World. What Mystics knew for ages, Modern Science is catching
up with, as their materialistic efforts are spiralling out of control.

In the **Beginning**, We'll start with profound Inner observation and
see how this translates to the God question. This understanding will
lead Us to the logical evolutionary tree of Our Soul's Journey.
Then, We will examine the Outer World of Matter while
further venturing through some Epic Magic of the **Universe**!

Arriving on the Earth, We'll be going through a **Human** Story, with
Our original capabilities and Our psychological dreams & **Illusion**s,
while the simplicity of the Truth is always Present & Aware of Our
every breath. Thus, by wisely moving forward, the atmosphere
changes, as We start **Travelling, Letting Go,** and **Awakening**
to healing poetic **Nature** and illuminous **Consciousness**.

We will end up with a Raw overview of the present
situation in **The World** and become inspired by
The Global Transformation of Humanity!

As You read, I recommend that You pause after every sentence,
every emptiness, to contemplate the deeper wisdom that it
points out. Since many are philosophical and allegorical,
I encourage You to take a Conscious breath after every
entry, and notice for Yourself the Truth of the statements.

We'll also question many beliefs here, and they should
all be put under the Conscious scrutiny of the Presence.

I use the terms Consciousness, God, Pure Consciousness,
Being, Beingness, Stillness, and Awareness with the same base
meaning. They are, however, differentiated for a broader linguistic
tapestry, for the beauty of literature, and to show how all religions,
traditions, and teachings point to this same Eternal Present Truth:
Consciousness.

You will notice many words starting with a Capital letter in order to
emphasise their importance. Or, in terms of individual and collective
personhood, I address Your and Our Divine Essence with Conscious
respect in this Spiritual endeavour. Some words are written entirely in
a LARGE or special font, showing the significance of the statement.

The shape of the text itself has an aesthetic look to keep narrations
flowing. I wrote it as a series of insightful narratives, information,
teachings, arguments, criticisms, and entries of poetic inspiration.

Most of the titles consist of several themes, and the actual
title signifies the main one. Almost every title includes
certain Conscious and Spiritual practices. I invite You to
read these passages open-heartedly, and the simplicity of
the teaching will arise as You feel it Within Yourself, as the
One undeniable experience of knowing, as the Self-awareness.

However, some verses are purely included for *poetical
purposes* – as a way of flavouring or loosening
up the subjects in that chapter or title.

I recommend reading this book while immersed in Nature!

Find that place away from the grid, where You feel
safe & free, without interruption, where You can
Let Go of the World by Abiding as Consciousness,
the place outside Time, where You're One with Nature,
whether in a forest, on a shoreline, or under the night sky.

Just one last thing before You start reading!
If You haven't already, watch this trailer-type of
inspiration, which is made specifically as a fly-through
visual birth and imagination of the Consciousness'
Universal incarnation of Our localised Earth perception.

It truly helps You appreciate the Vastness that
We're about to venture through, as a compilation and
direct vision of Our general ideas of the spectacular
nature of Life's infinite manifestations, within this
Grand Cosmic Voyage of endless Intoxications.

And turn the volume up for the full Universal impact !

CONSCIOUSNESS & The WORLD - Narrations of AWAKENING 2022

* * *

Now, Enjoy the Journey
and the Beauty of this

EXISTENTIAL PHILOSOPHY
and
SPIRITUAL INSPIRATION

There is an Entire Universe out There
Experiencing Itself as Conscious Beings
That is Yourself
On the Surface of this Planet
Right Here & Now

As Peace
As Love

CHAPTER 1

BEGINNING

Beginning

In the Beginning, there was Light of Consciousness;
It gave Rise to Vibration, Energy & Matter, through
which We experience Life as Pure Beingness.

The only way Light can find its way home is to
superimpose an entire range of the visible spectrum on itself,
with all the dimensions of dreaming in thoughts. But as the
ego dies, all the kingdoms of the mind will be known to Us,
thus, proving the All-seeing eye as Infinite Consciousness.

How We have been in Love with Creation; We helped
hold the Frequency of Its World-full duality.

You Are Perfection of Universal Magnitude in the
Act of Conscious Learning for Precious Self-Knowledge.
The Greatest Gift You Will Ever Experience Is Pure Consciousness!

*It is within this quality of presence that all other miracles of Life can be
felt, engaged, and manifested; as Our Higher Self is all about the Positive
Transformative Influential States of Oneness, which are always Here,
enjoying the many experiences of This needed virtual separateness.*

By sparing the reality of comprehending, there is no duality!

Now, at the High point of Freedom, We remember, again,
the Essence of Life and choose to Abide as Beingness of I

*   *   *

*Who You Are, is ultimately enveloped within the Awareness,
and the two are never separated, only the idea of You,
but the Self remains – it has always been Here*

You

Upon examining the True nature of the Self, One finds No Real You
as an independent entity. There is only Recognition, Observation,
or Awareness as apparent localised Consciousness. There is nothing
personal about it, and nobody can claim possession or special access to
Consciousness, as Consciousness is unbound and inherently unlimited.

The main thing that gives You a sense of Yourself is the thoughts about
Yourself and the very belief that thoughts add a private meaning to You,
which in turn enhances Your independent sense of Self. There is nothing
wrong with thoughts though. It is thoughtness clinging to thoughts
about itself, in a circle or self-empowering ideas that create the
feeling of Ourselves, and that infamous entity, the ego.

Nobody will judge You for the thoughts appearing within Your
awareness, but thoughts themselves can be a judgment of instant
Karma that is overlooking the sacredness of pure being: God. To
sin means to *miss the mark*, to ignore God by being unconscious.

The beginning of freedom is not identifying with thoughts,
which leads to peace where thoughts won't arise as much.
And non-attachment to Yourself is the core freedom from
which One doesn't attach to people, objects, ideas. By resting
in peace, feeling the love in Your heart, being that unbound
joy, We stop the need to seek fulfillment outside in The World.

From a Conscious view, thoughts are no different to rocks,
plants, dreams, or anything that is an objective experience.
The only difference is in the mindfully created privatised
deviations of thoughts' perpetuating belief in separation.
When We observe matter under extreme magnification, We
find it empty. Similarly, all outside appearances are created
by electrical signals interpreted in Our brains within
the Consciousness' localised perception.

We could say that nothing outside really exists, but We can't say that Consciousness doesn't 'exist.' Consciousness is the very Knowing which claims the existence or nonexistence of apparent reality. Therefore, We can only say that Existence's appearance is illusory, finite, and temporary. And We can draw the same conclusion when observing Our existence, in body, mind, thoughts, and feelings.

Consciousness is the only lasting quality as the observance behind every perceptual appearance, the constant watcher.

You could be a microscopic or GALACTIC-sized person and see a different set of realities. You could have an Out-of-body experience and still witness visual & sensory perceptions. Or You could dream of a convincing World and fully believe it.

The very fact that We experience Our own point of attention suggests God is the One Awareness who gave birth to such an independent sense of experiencing to know Himself. We are Individual aspects of the Creator.

In the same way, as there is no difference between Consciousness & Air, there is no difference between God, Consciousness, Air, and Us. We're the intrinsically innermost knowing of surrounding appearances. We're a Space allowing Existence to appear outside of Ourselves as temporary creation. Only so We can recognise the Source of It in Us; as Us; as It Is; as Is IS;
as IS IS

*   *   *

Nothing is Something; Something is Nothing,
both of them Are, both of them Is, both are One.
Something/Nothing never leaves the Oneness.
You can't destroy that which is never created.
You can't born that which has no opposites

Isness

Nothing exists outside Consciousness,
nothing can claim independence from IS.

For there to be Nothing, there must be
Something which Nothing can be the opposite to,
where Nothing can be Known against Something.
And there must be Consciousness aware of this
Nothingness, this Somethingness.

Therefore, both Nothing & Something must exist,
since Nothing is itself Something, so it can't not exist.
Their existence is always known in Consciousness, as
Consciousness can never be absent from anything.

In fact, Consciousness Gives Rise to Everything.
Where Everything, therefore Something or Nothing,
only appears as a secession of Consciousness' knowing
of itself, in the ever-expanding circles of recognition of itself.

In this way, Consciousness knows Itself in Something or Nothing,
for it doesn't have an independent existence outside of Itself.
Thus, Consciousness can only exist in Itself, and there must
be something in which Consciousness can recognise its
own existence. It must justify itself by knowing Itself by
knowing something other than itself. Through doing this,
it recognises Itself, and it does this by Knowing Thyself.

It does it in Itself, as Itself, from Itself, within Itself,
for it is Itself and can't be anything other than Itself.
So it only knows itselfness by being selfless Itself.

This Isness of Itself is the only thing Consciousness
can attribute to Itself, for In Itself, Is the Isness of Itself.

24

For these reasons of endless rotation of Beingness in Itself, it
serves Us better if We, for the sake of the language barrier
and of Understanding the True Nature of Consciousness,
decide to stop this ever-so-deepening cycle of creation
& Self-recognition in Waking, Dreaming, Sleeping,
by simply stating that Consciousness IS.

For the same reason, We don't need God Z;
who God Y created; who was created by God X;
who created... and all the way to A, where We
need to start from the End, or from the Start again.

We can purposefully & usefully talk about One Singular
ISness of Consciousness, and in that knowing, recognise
the possibilities of its infinite separation into BIG & small,
as the Fractal Pattern of the Mandelbrot Set shows.

As We realise the Somethingness, the Nothingness, and the
ISness of Everything that is appearing within Consciousness,
We don't need to go any further into details here. Our
only concern should be this innermost recognition
of Being, of Presence, of Stillness.

That is where We rest in God,
as Consciousness.
For Consciousness Is
resting as God,
in Us

*   *   *

In The Beginning...

*there is no beginning
nor ending*

Dreaming of Creation

I was Sleeping with Existence, Dreaming of
Universes, and Waking up with Creation.

I was Walking with Dinosaurs,
Living through Ages of History,
and Being One with Nature,
where I Conversed with the Sun.

Then I Remembered Everything,
All of Our Lives Throughout
Dimensions of Time! I Saw how
We are an Instrument of God,
a Divine Point in Space; Spirit,
by which He Knows Himself,
through His Own Creation.

A Supreme Being, Architect
of Matrix, Alpha & Omega of
Existence, One Infinite Creator.

Thus, all Matter is in Consciousness,
all Living Creatures are Sentient & Aware.

You Exist to Co-create Subtleties of Experience;
an Intricate details of various Shapes & Forms.

This Enigma is so Vast in its Complexity that
the Power of the Maker truly Surpasses all
Human and Existing Understandings!

Yet, He is Always Here,
As the Nature of
Your Being

God is tHere

Since the dawn of Man, since time immemorial, since The Fall, Humans have viewed reality in Separation. This subject-object perception caused a making up of explanations for the unknown phenomenon, which gave rise to belief through thought forms about 'supernatural' events, often trying to explain purely natural occurrences, causing World creation myths and legends of Gods. Such mixed-up, covered, and fused perception made Us overlook Consciousness as primary to Existence, to Self. With that, Humans have substituted Consciousness for God.

They made him something outside of Them, a projected relationship of attributed glorifications, fears, and desires. Therefore, God must be as LARGE as the Universe, making Us small and insignificant in comparison. They also made him a living being, incomprehensible, leaving Us obeying his written word. Obviously, many Souls are playing God's character, channelling Their mysterious ways through Man, with a primarily beautiful, profound message, but They ascribe misleading authorship. This process is entirely understandable, and how else could it be in this solid reality. Parallel to this separation-evolution, some traditions have known the ultimate truth all along. Like Nondual understanding, which became more popular through teachings of Advaita Vedanta tradition, and other mostly eastern individuals who inquired about this Self-aware knowing of reality and put it into literary works such as Tao Te Ching and Ashtavakra Gita.

If We, Humans, can realise Our True nature as Consciousness, and within that have no intent or need to interfere with Existence, which is the case with many sages, yogis and individuals who have truly found liberation from the ego, then who are We to say that God would have any existential agenda Himself? He wouldn't, and He didn't! Otherwise, He wouldn't be the God, but merely a powerful Universal Being, similar to the Q character from Star Trek. And We know how that would go. We cannot add personality to God, since Consciousness has no persona, and God can only be Infinitely Conscious. The God wouldn't care about being a God. To add personality to God is to deny Him! Therefore, He, or She, or IT, is eternally silent and forever unconditionally

loving, so much so that He, She, or IT will never interfere in creation.
God is All that tHere IS! He is synonymous with Being; Consciousness.
In fact, *God & Consciousness are One! There is no separation between
the two, as there is no separation between Us & Them.
The only difference is Our thoughts of separation.*

To equate God with Consciousness is to put Him on the highest pedestal,
on the first & foremost place in Existence. And not even that, because God
doesn't really exist, rather; *Existence Godz – as Our Love when Awakened,
but as Beingness, is the Pure Consciousness!*

When talking about Creation, We should use a different language,
since We must separate God from Existence, and Creation.
For this purpose of the Highest Reasoning, God needed to
separate Himself from Existence. He needed to wash His hands,
so to speak, of being accountable and, thus, free from Creation.

*"The manifest universe is the body of God...
all people are incarnations of the One Spirit."* **Ernest Holmes**

Spirit is then God's Emissary and is Love Manifested as the Universe, as
Existence, as personality and apparent Life of All Beings within Creation.
Spirit is the way We shift the blame & existential burden away from God,
&, in this way, We can have a personal & creative relationship with Them.
Spirit is the Ultimate Knowledge, the Highest Wisdom, the Greatest
Intelligence, an Eternal Inspiration! Spirit is the Hive Mind, the Divine
Matrix, the Akashic Records, the Source Field, the Relationship with God.

Of course, these are all Spiritual existential philosophies, and there could
be countless other ways of Spiritual manifestation within the Universe,
or none. And all are an experience in Consciousness.

Again, there is no need to go into this any further. It is sufficient to
know the Fundamental Truth to Everything, which is Consciousness,
and all else is an acute way of explaining Consciousness' many, but
ultimately One & Only singular nature: The Pure Beingness

The Nature of Reality

Primal Nature of Existence, BEINGNESS,

IS THE CONSCIOUSNESS !

NOTHING Exists Outside of that KNOWING !

HERE, Originated Supreme Creator : GOD !

And the Universal Source Essence of LIFE : SPIRIT !

Whose Emanating LIGHT is : LOVE !

It then Created the MATRIX for Experience : THE UNIVERSE !

And Within It : SPACE-TIME, MATTER/ENERGY/FORCE !

SPIRIT Separated Thyself into an Infinite number of
Personalised Versions of Itself, and with that Gave
Rise to the Medium of Our Individuality : SOUL !

It Furthermore Played the Game of Creation,
Combining the existing ELEMENTS into : LIVING CELLS !

This NATURAL WORLD is : The GARDEN of EDEN !

In order to Experience the Existence in All its Fullness,
another SPARK of LIFE was Conceived as the Carrier for
the Soul Senses, and gave Birth to a BODY : HUMAN !

As The Story then goes,

HUMAN Lived in ONENESS with GOD, as NATURE !

IT then Developed a Private Independent Sense of
Self-Awareness : Mind, Thoughts, Emotions : EGO !

Ego in Itself as an Individualised way of Experience
Dreamed & Imagined the Polarities : GOOD and EVIL !

That, in turn, fuelled the entire new tapestry of Separation !

So Those who Remembered Their UNITY with Creation,
Their Original Link to GOD, as the way of staying in
the Primal State of Being, Inspired by Their Soul,
set the Foundation for : SPIRITUALITY ! And
its institutionalised version : Religion !

To conclude :

Consciousness Godz,
God Abides by the Spirit,
Spirit Knows as the Soul,
a Soul Dreams the Mind,
a Mind Dances the Body,
a Body Feels a Thought,
Thoughts Evoke Emotions,
and Life Envelops Them
All in Love !

YOU Are The PURE CONSCIOUSNESS !

The Essence of GOD, SPIRIT !

Experiencing this Universe of Creation

through LIFE in LOVE,

as Body, as SOUL

Existence

"Reality is merely an illusion, albeit a very persistent one." **Albert Einstein**

How does Existence exist? How can it be so accurate and persistent?

Since We are Conscious, how does this reality, this mind illusion continue? Shouldn't it simply dissolve like a lucid dream, after every Conscious recognition, after every thought? Why don't We sometimes wake up in some different Universe, some other reality?

But no, somehow, We're stuck so deep in this dream that it seems as eternal as the Universe and as solid as matter. The obvious existence of Our collective experience of the Universe proves that We're indeed stuck so deeply in the dream that We even call it a reality: *"Something that is neither derivative nor dependent but exists necessarily."*

We also call it Life, and We even think that this is all there is to the Existence, that there is only this Life. People who believe in something more than this reality or the afterlife are called religious or spiritual. They base Their assumptions on belief, on shared intuition, which is mainly the product of a Mystic's Life, around which They base Their faith. But Those Mystics base Their certainties on deep personal knowledge. Or simply on the rawest natural understanding of this reality One could have, since They show little or no signs of illusory behaviour such as an egoic sense of self, but perceive reality consciously as It Is.

Now, why would the absence of ego or thoughts give any credence to making claims about reality, and does it? In the end, scientists who observe and study the illusory appearance of reality have all the data, and We credit Them with understanding the Universe. And Mystics are more responsible for that philosophical meaning of Existence.

"The concepts of spirituality is generally just the physics we haven't understood yet." **Nassim Haramein**

The more scientists look into the solidity of matter, the less solid
it seems. We know that matter is not solid. It is an information
field that Our senses decode and perceive as a solid appearance.

"Everything we call real is made of things that cannot be regarded as real."
Niels Bohr

Many scientists are turning into Mystics because the only certainty
They observe about reality is the fact that there is observance itself.

"I regard consciousness as fundamental. I regard matter as derivative from consciousness. We cannot get behind consciousness. Everything that we talk about, everything that we regard as existing, postulates consciousness."
Max Planck

You don't observe as Consciousness; Consciousness observes as You!

The mind, the thoughts, the tools, the Science, and Humanity have
developed through the belief & observation of their illusory appearance
to finally recognise themselves as Consciousness. We thus know that
only Consciousness exists, only Consciousness Is, and We'll explain
the reality of The World within that shifting paradigm.

"All matter is merely energy condensed to a slow vibration, we are all one consciousness experiencing itself subjectively, there is no such thing as death, life is only a dream, and we are the imagination of ourselves." **Bill Hicks**

The New Science will be that one of the True Self; Consciousness

*   *   *

"It is paradoxical, yet true, to say, that the more we know, the more ignorant we become in the absolute sense, for it is only through enlightenment that we become conscious of our limitations. Precisely one of the most gratifying results of intellectual evolution is the continuous opening up of new and greater prospects." **Nikola Tesla**

Structure of the Universe

What is Our World made of?

The Universe is made of Atoms,
which have a Nucleus in the Centre
made of Protons & Neutrons, which are
made of Quarks that are made of Strings.

The Nucleus is orbited by Electrons at such a
distance that it makes Atoms virtually Empty!

Atoms have a certain number of Particles that come
in 92 shapes or Elements, which make up the Periodic
table (Humans have created 24 more elements).

When exposed through a Prism, their Light
gives a unique Rainbow signature or Spectrum.
Their Photons are particle Units of Light.

Elements are used by Cells of Plants & Animals,
getting Instructions from their DNA to Create
Molecules of those Living Organisms.

All Living Cells are traceable to the First Single One!

All Elements and Earth that We are made of
were Created In the Suns and the Massive
Explosions in the Universe – mainly the Big Bang.

We know of 4 fundamental Forces in the Universe:
Electromagnetism, Gravity, Strong and Weak Force.

And Effects like Sound, Heat, Fusion, Fission, Radiations,
Rays, Wormholes, Black Holes, Dark Matter & Dark Energy.

The primary properties of Matter are Mass, Spin, and Charge.
All Matter has equal & opposite Antimatter,
with the two always cancelling each other out,
except for a few atoms that are left,
which is today All the Matter of Our Universe.

Empty Space or Vacuum isn't empty but is Full of Action and
particles constantly appearing & disappearing, or borrowing.

There are also many Dimensions (11).
Probably a Multiverse or Infinity.
Possibly Parallel Realities as well.

Everything in the Universe exists in perfect Equilibrium,
and nothing is excluded, where every part, however small it
may be, is one piece of the puzzle of the LARGER whole.

The Universe has some inherent traits of behaviour, such as:
Laws, Vibration, Inflation, Information, Vortex, Pattern, Wave,
Chaos, Order & Disorder, Reflection, Refraction, Entropy, Explosion,
Extension, Inversion, the Hologram, and the Uncertainty principle.

To Discover, Measure, and Theorise all of this took thousands
of years, but most of the Scientific progress happened
in the last 120 years and is speeding up exponentially.

*"Science is a systematic enterprise that builds and organizes knowledge
in the form of testable explanations and predictions about the universe."*

We use some interesting ways of describing the Universe:
Natural Science of Life/Biology, Physical Science such as Quantum
Mechanics, and lots of Big numbers: Thousand, Million, Billion,
Trillion, Quadrillion, Quintillion, Sextillion, Septillion, Octillion,
Nonillion, Decillion, Undecillion, Duodecillion, Tredecillion,
Graham Number-illion, Google, Google Plex,
Imaginary, Zero, One, and Infinity.

Science has many branches, and it's the best Instrument
in understanding the Structure of the Universe.

*"The greatest achievements of science is to allow humanity to
realize that our world is comprehensible. Through science, rational
thinking, we can understand how the universe works."* **Jim Al-Khalili**

Fortunately, We don't just have to *Shut up and calculate!*
For who does the observations: CONSCIOUSNESS !

*"Consciousness poses the most baffling problems in the science of the mind.
There is nothing that we know more intimately than conscious experience,
but there is nothing that is harder to explain."* **David Chalmers**

Hence the profundity by which All Experience Is Known!
And *The Hard Problem,* or *Impossible,* as **Peter Russell** put it, is:
*"How does something as unconscious as the matter of the brain, can
ever give rise to something as immaterial as Consciousness?"*

The Very Fact That We Are In Consciousness and
Can Reflect & Witness The World Around Us,
**IS THE GREATEST MYSTERY
IN EXISTENCE**

*   *   *

*There are 10,000 Grains of Sand in One Handful.
That is more than the Number of Stars We can See in the Night Sky.*

*But there are more Stars in the Universe than all
the Grains of Sand in the Entire World.
And wait, it gets better!*

*There are more Molecules in a Drop of Water
than Sand in the World or Stars in the Universe.
So there is an Entire Universe in a Drop of Water*

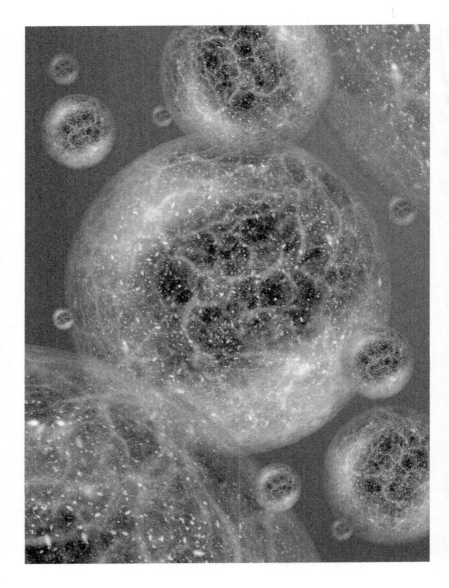

CHAPTER 2

UNIVERSE

Large-Scale Structure

We're moving at Warp Speed, after
travelling for circa Eternity as it seems.
To finally arrive at the Largest distance
from Us, and that much closer to Infinity.

And Now, We're witnessing the most Spectacular,
most Impressive, goose-bump-inducing, dramatical,
bone-chilling, most Outstanding and Grandest Image,
the Most Magnificent Site in the Whole of the Existence,
in this Theoretical View of the Observable Universe:

UNIVERSE'S LARGE-SCALE STRUCTURE !

And this is where You Stop & Stand in Awe!
This is where You weep, You cry!
For This Is Where We Live,
This is Our Home,

This is Our GOD !

If We're going to Feel Him
anywhere, it better be Here & Now!
For this is His Divine Cosmic Blueprint of
Quintessence, on a UNIVERSAL SCALE of Things.

What We See is a Structure of a Thread-like Tapestry.
Here, every dot is not a Galaxy. It is a Supercluster
containing thousands of individual Galaxies.

*It's the Greatest Soul-Ascending the Universe-Creating
Symphony of All Times! It's the GOD Thyself.
Here, We Exist in more than One Place
and more than One Space in Time.*

Now, all this Universal scale of things, all the mind-bending
distances and huge spans of time, are nothing more than a thought,
an image in Our mind. It is not accurate; it is imaginary, projected.

It is a theory, as everything else that
Consciousness can't notice directly also is.

But as We build these ideas on Our Scientific investigations,
they are the most beautiful tool, the most awe-inspiring
imagination helping Us Understand Our place in Existence.

They are so vast, so distant & undefined, that they are
the closest & best catalyst for Consciousness expansion.

"For small creatures such as we, the vastness is bearable only through love."
Carl Sagan

And This is what I want You to do!
I want You to expand Your Vision, View, and mind's Eye.
I want You to allow Yourself to Be ONE with Existence,
with God; be as One Love, as Consciousness.

For just look at The Large-Scale Structure!
It is identical to the neuron image of Our brain.
So the Universe Is the Super-brain of God, to say!
With Us being its Conscious Soul Essence.

This type of understanding will bring about the
Awakening in Consciousness We desperately Now Need,
and the one which Our World is urgently begging for!

Let Us Expand Our Awareness of The World,
of the Universe, and Our Place In It All.

Let Us Allow for more
Consciousness

Final Frontier

Blackness, Consciousness, the Final Frontier!

These are the Voyages of Our ego's unconsciousness.
Their Mission: to blindly go where no mind has gone before.
To Reunite Itself with the One, in countless myriads of
blazing Suns, all under the illusion of Space & Time.

Darkness, the Absence of Light!
The most common sight in the Universe.
So Distant & Vast that if You found Yourself in the
middle of 99% of the Universe, it would be Pitch Black.
That is how precious to Us, Light & Matter are!

Complete Darkness is Pure Consciousness, an absence
of Anything. Therefore Nothing, not even Awareness,
is there, except in its fundament, like a Field of
Possibility which Span the Entire Existence.

Become friends with Darkness.
It is All that Is, Was, and Ever Will Be!
For it is the only thing that exists.
Everything else is an Illusion of form & matter, energy
& vibration. And that is empty also, in voidless essence.

When What Is IS, then Blackness Unites, as Dark Matter Does,
as boundless Consciousness Creating & Infiltrating every
Quantum of Thought, every Spark of Atomic Quark.

Black is The New Old Natural, where The Great Unknown
becomes the most Familiar & Intimate Sense, The Self which
never Goes, it never Dies. It Ties Us in the Absence of
Death, but Thrives as the Luminous
Dark of Life

Eyes of the Universe

Let Us say You were to take a journey across the Universe,
as if You were in Star Trek or Star Wars, encountering
endless Worlds, species, anomalies, and so many destinies.

That would give You an overwhelming insight into the Existence;
it would make You wise, Spirit-like. You wouldn't be a Human travelling;
You would be the Consciousness of the Universe looking back on Itself.

Just seeing the Earth from orbit would change Your Worldview and
expand Your Awareness, let alone Trekking around the Universe.

We're such Spirit already Now; Our range of motion is just a lot less.

We go to work, stay at home with Our families, and sometimes We
go a bit farther, so We have the experience of Our localised sense of
perception. And We have to start somewhere to get that frame of
reference, distance & space, of Us & Them, to Enlarge Our Vision,
to Telescope Our View of the World, to Expand Our Awareness
to Include Everyone & Everything in Existence!

And You don't even have Consciousness but exist Within It.
You live to become Conscious. Otherwise, You're unconscious.
You're not aware of the Existence, which means You don't live;
all is just happening, and that makes no intuitive sense, does it?

"An unexamined life is not worth living." **Socrates**

We don't know if the large Universe even exists; We've never been there.
We only see this part, and maybe this is the only part there is to him.
But the idea and measurements of the Universe give Us the simplest
picture of Consciousness. Consciousness is the Vastness in
which the Universes framework appears.

The Universe is the Picture, the Dream in Consciousness.
All the Stars and Galaxies appear in the Eyes of Consciousness.
Flying through the Universe is moving through those Eyes.

*Here, We lose Ourselves to intergalactic immensity. We surrender Our
identities to the majesty of Universes' enormity and find God as the
lasting Cosmological remedy in the birth pangs of deathless infusion.*

tHere, Space & Time are the by-products of Our brain & mind,
of the Consciousness' experience of incalculable deviations.

Pondering the Meaning of it All and Knowing the Universe
is the Grandest thing Humans can achieve!

And Being Self-aware is
the Greatest Thing
We Can Be
As
We Are

*   *   *

*We Imagine
how it is Out tHere,
in the Infinity of Existence.*

*While through Us,
Infinity Imagines,
how it is
to Be,*

*Here
&
Now*

Nebula in the Mood

Our Celestial Space Saga is Continuing!

We're flying through the Mesmerising Bioluminescent
Nebula. She is a Direct Descendant of the Big Bang
Mother and Now Pregnant with the Space Potency of
the Real Universal Magic of Radiation, in Action!

These eternally promised Sparks of Stars are
becoming more unstable in the Womb of Creation.
All preceded by Comets of Future's Premonition
and following the justified excitement
when We witnessed:

The Greatest Fireworks Display in the Universe!

An Outstanding Singularity Explosion of Supernovae Stars!

Presented in many Types & Flavours of the Light Signature,
like Gamma-ray bursts and Super-luminous ones too.

Such Power is so Great that they Outshine
an entire Host Galaxy with their Blinding Light.
Introducing Us to the Brilliant Life in the making of
Space, and all happening in this Stellar Fabric of Time.

Therein lies the Origin of Our Cosmic Nebula in the Mood!

She is impregnated by the Collective Powers of the Universal Forces,
a Tantric Dance of Matter, which delivers its vapour like Energy,
in the form of Lovemaking by Clouds of Dust,
consisting of many types of Particles
and every kind of Gas.

And Now, She is a GIGANTIC Nursery for
Giving Birth to Newly-created Photon Life, in
the swirling Placentas of fast-spinning Proto-Stars.

Her Nucleosynthesis is a Shining Light, like a new-born
baby's innocent cry, of beautiful and promising
billions of years-long Thermally Heated Hearts.

Filled with:
Childhood of utmost Fascination with Creation,
of Adrenalin pumped Nuclear Energy of Fusion.

Adolescent of the Never-exhausting Power of its
Glowing longevity cycle, depending on the Mass.

And Adulthood of Fission!

Whereby all Matter then Transforms into Energy for
the Next Generation of Now-forming Constellation Stars.

As part of this Grand Cosmological Event, reminiscent
of Our Soul's journey of infinite Births & Deaths.

Where the Essence of God passes down the
endless chain to the next Generations of
forever evolving Cosmological Selves.

In all shapes & forms of Biological
& Inanimate Presence of Being,

in Multiversal Universally

shared

Stuff of Life

A <u>Galactic Home</u>

The Universe is Our Home at LARGE. It is the
ultimate mystery of Life, synonymous with Consciousness,
and with that, a source flow of Infinite & Universal inspiration.

Earth's atmosphere is a thin layer separating Us from the Universe,
from the endless freezing coldness, a vast eternal spatial silence,
and occasional burning hot spots of the spinning Galaxy disk
comprising billions of flaming Suns, surrounding
the Supermassive Black hole's wheel of giving Life.

These Cosmic beacons of rotating light, electromagnetic fields,
and radiation of the Galactic nucleus as pulsars, blazars, magnetars,
and quasars are dancing to the rhythm of the torque spin.

All these Universal forces of energetic motion are the engines of
creation and are solely responsible for the grand spectacle of forming
density points, exoplanets, asteroids, and comets as wandering stars.

As the primordial soup of gas & dust forms the Solar Systems,
the essence of the Universe is biologically shaped and gives rise
to the organic matter, through which Conscious participants
can reflect and appreciate the Miracle

*   *   *

*"I know that the molecules in my body are
traceable to phenomena in the cosmos.
We are all connected; To each other,
biologically. To the earth, chemically.
To the rest of the universe atomically."*

Neil deGrasse Tyson

I have a Vision

...about Human & Alien Life coexisting peacefully!

If You think We are Alone in the Universe,
that is a huge comprehension failure.

It's more likely that We're surrounded by intelligent Life,
waiting on Us to Wake Up from Our global dreams of ego, to
look around and realise that We need to Think, Feel, and Exist more
consciously. To care for the Environment and Our Fellow Humans, and
to start working together collectively as One Human Civilisation.

*"We're reaching the point where the Earth will have to end the burden
we've placed on her, if we don't lift the burden ourselves."* **Steven Greer**

And when that happens, They will introduce Themselves publicly.
But before that, We need to learn to function normally & sustainably
within Our Own Communities, on Our Own Planet. Then, They'll be
looking at Us as worthy members of the Interstellar Community,
the Galactic Federation, and the Intergalactic Family of Beings.

All of this will happen eventually, my Dear Humans!

It may have already happened; We may have already
had advanced Humans before, who left the Earth and this
Solar system in The Search of Their Mysterious Stellar Ways.

*"Two possibilities exist: either we are alone in the Universe or
we are not. Both are equally terrifying."* **Sir Arthur C. Clarke**

All these options need consideration. We must put them into
the Awareness of Our Nation. Not just as Sci-Fi movies,
but as the inevitable consequence of expanding the Global,
Solar, Galactic, and Universal interest of Our species.

We can then allow for a more open & sharing Civilisation.
One working tirelessly to Save Itself and Explore the Stars!

Imagine Yourself before the Universe, before the Time & Space, without body & thoughts, just pure being – awareness, knowing; Consciousness.
That's what it means to be at the nexus point before manifestation.

To imagine anything, thought is required; an intention of
creation and The World appear as a dream in God's mind.

We now exist in a multiple if not infinite layering of imaginary
sustainments or dimensions, and the density of it We call matter.

"If you reject the infinite, you are stuck with the finite, and the finite is parochial... the best explanation of anything eventually involves universality, and therefore infinity." **David Deutsch**

If You've ever wondered how it is Out There Infinitely,
in the Vastness of Space, in the Universe's Enormity,
what types of species live there, and What They do...

Well, Welcome Home, for You are that Answer!

Those far away Alien species are asking Themselves the same.

So This is How it Feels to Live anywhere in the Universe.
The Earth and Human Civilisation is the Answer!
We are One of those far-away Alien species, in Our
Image and After Our Likeness. We Are Aliens

*   *   *

*To stand Aware in front of Civilisation is both
a Tremendous Burden and the Greatest Privilege!
But above All, an Infinite Freedom*

Imagine

Imagine if You Lived on some simple World,
like the Little Prince Asteroid, and I told You:

You know, there is a distant, strange, and mesmerising Globe out there!
Where the Giant Grass Grows, filled with all types of Insects & Creatures
moving around, and an Enormous Liquid Substance covers the entire
World, inhabited by Countless Shapes of Swimming Forms.

The Skies are Greeted by Flying Lines, Combining the
Two Worlds into One Living & Breathing Sphere!
And that is just the beginning of an incredible
Natural Assortment found on that Planet.

You would be in disbelief, wondering how such diversity
could exist and how it could ever come into being.
What would create such a Miracle of Life?
Something beyond all known imagination, which surely
cannot possibly exist, and by all means, it never will.

And yet, You and Me, We Live in such a World

*   *   *

"Under the stars each night
I wonder do stairs go there?
I'm lonely driving behind the wheel
Can't get no where
I can't seem to get it right
I'm only just a man of steel
...Is there a place?

And under the stars tonight
I wonder if someone cares
I'm lonely, that's the way I feel
Can't feel no stairs
I've gotten a real ad-heist
I'm only just a man of steel
...There is a place..."

Franck Black, Man of Steel

<u>Stars</u>

Humans are a part of something far Greater and more
Spectacular than Our day-to-day Life would acknowledge.

First, to be a Conscious Being is already the most
Magnificent Phenomenon of Being that Exists!

To make it clearer to You, look at Nature: vegetation, animals,
matter, the Universe. It is all there, yes! But can You talk to them?
Can You Live in a close social circle and have a meaningful relationship
with them? Can You have an intelligent and Conscious exchange?

And look at Us, Humans! We can communicate with language.
We can be fully aware of Ourselves and Others, and We can have
a meaningful Soul connection to Other members of Our species.

If You were to find Yourself alone, even on another planet,
such as being alone on the dead Mars, let's say, it would make You
appreciate the importance We have as Conscious & Social Beings.

If You could see the Alive Earth from Space for a few moments,
it would change Your Life completely.

Do You see how simple & obvious but profound a fact this is?
How Responsible This Self-Aware Ability Makes Us!

We have the Chance & Responsibility to Take Care
of The World, as nobody else will, nor can they.

You Are Alive, Aware, Sentient, and Conscious!
You can think, feel, observe, reason, philosophise,
and You can transcend the experience by going within.
That makes Us a Supreme species and certainly capable
of taking care of Our every deed & action.

So I'll tell You this again!
This current state of Being, as Human Civilisation, is the
most Magnificent Existential Phenomenon in the Universe!
For it is the Only One We Know and Are Aware of.

*"The cosmos is within us. We are made of star-stuff.
We are a way for the universe to know itself."* **Carl Sagan**

We are in the inheritance of such Infinity, of the 13.8 billion years of
the Universal Heritage, as different expressions of Consciousness
manifested, where Consciousness is an Eternity in a moment.

*Mind & Body are like Parallel Universes. Anything happening
in the Mental Universe must leave traces in the Physical One.*

The Ultimate fate of the Universe is relatively known;
*Unconsciousness, all Civilisations, the Universe, an entire Existence
will naturally return to Consciousness. All the noise and thoughts will
stop, all bodies will die, all technology will shut down, all Suns will
burn out, Planets will cool down, all Souls will meet in Spirit and abide
in God, and only Consciousness will remain. It will be, as It IS.*

And so We will not abandon this Journey Now,
We'll not forget Our True nature!

We will Reorganise & Return,
to the STARS

*   *   *

*"When God decided that it was time for your Soul to come to Earth,
the Universe was crying because it knew that is losing its brightest Star,
and now still, if you look up to the skies, you can see Universe's tears
as it still cries for you, and now the brightest shine of your Soul
is brightening my World Here."* **Angie**

CHAPTER 3

HUMAN

The Story of Humanity

It is the Oldest Story in History!
Humans forgot Their True nature and
built a Civilisation whilst destroying Their Natural habitat.

If some out of hand & time catastrophe doesn't wipe Them out sooner,
the only way to survive (technology allowing) would be to move to
other Planets since it would already be too late for the Home Planet.

Or, They would assimilate with their aforementioned technology
and continue to live in the Complex Matrix Systems.

What are the chances that none of these scenarios happen?

The answer will always be One to Infinity, in favour of All Possibilities!

For if You invest in studying these subjects, You will know that
Reality is Simulated. That entire Existence is created by One
particle moving at an Infinite Speed or it is a Quantum Hologram.

Up until now, We've been studying the pixels of illusory appearance.

*"To consider consciousness an emergent property of brains is either
an appeal to magic or the mere labeling of unknown. In both cases,
precisely nothing is actually explained."* **Bernardo Kastrup**

As We discover more about both the Brain & the Universe's
holographic nature, We realise how *The Observer* (or *The Conscious
agent* as **Donald Hoffman** calls it) plays the primary role in this
Existential Mystery. We're discovering how Consciousness is the
only undeniable existence. Thus, *this is God's Dream, experiencing
itself through billions of individual unconscious Beings as well as the
few who have Awakened Their innate ability to step outside of the
thought-loop ego-created states of mind by becoming Self-aware.*

Now, what does it actually mean to know the Universe as a Simulation, a Hologram, as Conscious Realism, or as God's Dream? The answer is that it's to examine the Universe Consciously from Within; to be poetic & romantic in the Existential sense of grasping and understanding.

These ideas & terms, which We use to describe Humanity's existence in the Universe, are Our creations of interpretations. Consciousness & The Universe simply Are, as It IS, where the latter is an external projection of the former.

"The new discipline will be the study of the psychophysical nature of reality, that mysterious, interstitial space shimmering between mind and matter." **Dean Radin**

However, merely applying Our understanding and naming the laws doesn't serve to create, explain, or describe the Truth. If anything, it labels the illusion and entertains Our minds. All 'Laws of Nature' are changeable; they are not constant. Thus, only Consciousness can be the undeniable constant.

So whatever mechanism We and this World are subject to, there is only Consciousness, there is only Love.

I know that every blade of grass, every tree, animal, every drop of water, every photon of Light, every atom in the Universe is special, precious, has meaning, and is filled with Life. For this reason, every moment of Existence is in Consciousness

* * *

When You Create a Virtual Reality indistinguishable from Your World, the chances that You Yourself Live in the Artificial Construct known as this Cosmos of the Multiverse – backed by Simulated Reality Hypothesis, Holographic Universe Principle, and Multimodal user interface – are Infinity To None

Language

There are 7,000 languages spoken in the World today, and one could potentially learn any of them perfectly by studying the depth of their meaning. The key point here is the meaning, which We then put into sounds & voices, symbols, words, and grammar, to convey the details of each language's uniqueness. Many Natives have no written language; They pass Their tongue down verbally using hand signs and gestures. The need to sing & speak is inherent in Human Beings in general, thus any language is a natural progression of such vocal, and later thoughtness, engagement of the Human mind within The World.

Every language is in a state of constant change, depending on the progress of the culture or Civilisation that uses it. We create new words, forget the old ones, and adopt the former to explain the current situation. Proper use of language from a young age is like learning a habitual task, with most people doing it unintentionally. Due to Our social & cultural conditionings, We are predispositioned to think & speak a certain way. Instead of Us using language, language is using Us.

Our thoughts are not Our own, Our opinions are someone else's, and We believe that We are those thoughts; We think that We are Our minds. We have become the very mind, the same language that is meant to help Us to express the freedom We naturally feel as Sentient Beings. Our Awareness has been substituted for the mere voices in Our minds. With these communicative concepts limiting Our Lifetime's intellectual growth, this is the madness that has become Our reality.

"You have a voice in your head that keeps saying things, haven't you noticed." **Sam Harris**

We think how We speak, and We speak how We think!
Instead of expressing Our unique experience and communicating that authenticity in a wise & articulated way, We repeat the learned stereotypical phrases. We've turned Ourselves into people repeaters.

"Watch your thoughts, they become your words; watch your words, they become your actions; watch your actions, they become your habits; watch your habits, they become your character; watch your character, it becomes your destiny." **Lao Tzu**

This mindful trap is one reason why most people stop learning as soon as They have left public education. With this, Their Worldview becomes fixed. They shut down Their Soul. Their ego keeps Them in the clutches of ignorance, in chains of Self-denial, in fear of the unknown. But there is not, and there can't be, an end to knowledge as a whole, since the brain and mind aren't fixed. They're fluid and change throughout a Lifetime. Our minds are a never-ending maze of possibilities in comprehending worldly reality, thus True Education can't be the monotonous repetition of memorised sentences. Education must entail learning how to deal with practical tasks and *training the mind to think*.

The basic problem with language is that it confines Our understanding within its limitations. As such, it is helpful to know more than one language, as each one has different meanings, nuances, and they're not so easily interchangeable. For this reason, when We translate languages, We don't simply directly translate the words. Rather, We think about the meaning held within the words and context within the theme being discussed. And then We can choose the words & sentences in the other language that We deem as the most appropriate, closest words to correctly convey the intended meaning.
The further back in History We go, the more difficult it is to translate from one language to another since there are no perfectly matching meanings. So We must use the closest words and even make a leap of faith or apply Our interpretations. And that is the reason why ancient texts and bibles are not reliable sources of direct knowledge.

We must, therefore, rely on Our present understandings of the World to find the Universal truth in the only unchanging and ever-lasting wisdom, the aspect of Knowing that is identical to every Being in the Universe that is not subject to thought or language: the domain of Self-awareness.

That One & Only Universal Truth is Consciousness

Soul

The Human Being is an entity in a state of constant development!

That is what I call the Human Soul.
It is Our Awareness, Our Spirit, Our Life & Love.
It's Our Body, Nature, Animals, Medicine, Language, Science,
Feelings, Intuition, Spirituality, Religions, Beliefs, History, Literature,
Creativity, Arts, Culture, Intelligence, Knowledge, Philosophy, Wisdom,
Stories, Myths, Legends, Ideals, Morals, Values, Transcendence, GOD.

Values & Virtues are the Life qualities of Conscious Beings,
which promote the personal and general well-being of
society and the entire ecosystem that They inhabit.

The more of the Human Soul We forget, the more ancestral heritage
We lose. Since new generations are quicker to abandon the traditional
upbringing and values of Their grandparents & parents, society melts
further into the current stream of trends & styles. We're forgetting and
losing parts of Ourselves, that, in turn, speeds up modern evolution.

To Protect and Remember Our History is a Vital Part of Who We Are!
To have an Entire understanding of Who We Are & How We Got Here,
Is To Understand Our Place In The Great Scheme of Things.

That is the Sum-total of Our Evolving, Shared Existence.
And We should always Learn, Evolve, and Grow,
Personally & Collectively as a Civilisation.

The Greatest wisdom an Leap forward is to Share Your
Truest personal & Original experience. It's to be Yourself fully!

By diving deep down to the Basis of perceiving Existence,
Know You Are The Pure Consciousness,
Experiencing Itself As Unconditional Love!

*"Love is patient, love is kind. It does not envy, it does not boast, it is not proud.
It does not dishonour others, it is not self-seeking, it is not easily angered,
it keeps no record of wrongs. Love does not delight in evil but rejoices
with the truth. It always protects, always trusts, always hopes, always
perseveres. Love never fails."* **St. Paul 1 Corinthians 13**

*Share This Love Anywhere You Go, With Everyone You Meet,
Thus Remembering Them To Reawaken The Soul Essence.
Abide By The Grace You Have Inside,
Remain In The Peace You Are Within.
Be Aware of Each Breath-In,
Follow Through Every Breath-Out.
As There Is No Pain, There Is No Path.
All We Have Ever Been,
Eternal Presence,
Is Always HERE,
and Just Right
NOW*

*   *   *

This Existence is Mesmerising Dimensionality

*A Dance of Light, where
Many Worlds Theory Vs. Matter Flux Energy
=
Spirit-Shaping Synergy*

*An Infinite Tapestry Co-creating
Vibrational Fluid-Foam Tetragrammaton Super-Membranes*

*Universally Known by Us, as Inter-Galactic Scientists
Devotees of Our Heart's Luminosities
Fluorescently Sparkling & Reproducing*

The New YOU and The New ME

Heart

Your Heart is not just a blood-pumping muscle!
It is 5,000 times magnetically stronger than the brain.
As the Electromagnetic Emotional Right-from-Wrong Detector,
it shows You how it feels when You do or think something. Your Heart
should always be at peace; it should always be in calm & playful joy.

If it feels heavy & painful, which often reflects in the belly, Your
Heart is telling You that You're going against Yourself,
creating fear as another Emotional trigger and it's
Feeling You that You're ego-tripping.

"The less you open your heart to others,
the more your heart suffers."
Deepak Chopra

Listen to Your Heart's Intuition & Knowing!
Only when We express Our deepest Selves regardless
of circumstances shall We know the True Freedom & Joy.

Although, in essence, Consciousness is all there really & ever Is,
the Heart is a Sensational Centre that keeps having a physical
body, brain, mind, thoughts, feelings, and Soul, all these
aspects of Individual experience, together. Ergo,
keep Your mind in the Heart & literally so.
For Your brain is a Computer,
but Your Heart
is Love

*   *   *

Unconditional Love is the only Truth, and We Live that by treating
Everybody We meet with Kindness & Respect, thus having a clear conscience

Emotions

What is an Emotion or a Feeling? Are they the same? How can We
distinguish between things as elusive and as mixed-up as Emotions?
How do We make sense of them in amongst all the thoughts?
Can Emotions arise without thoughts through pure perception?

As with everything else in Life, We need to dissect all of
these sensations one by one, as whatever appears
within Consciousness occurs individually, one at a time.
Let's sit in peace, in stillness, and recognise everything that is
noticeable now as We focus Our attention on the present experience.

We are first aware of Our breath. So allow Yourself this observance of
breathing right now. Follow it In & Out, and notice different sensations
within Your body too.
I am sure some thoughts are also coming & going, and as Our attention
is drawn to them, Our focus is sucked into the mind, creating a loop of
dwelling, which We call thinking. We can't know Our next thoughts, so
We can't be sure what will arise next. We can only stay aware of whatever
arises. By practising conscious breathing, however, We become more &
more aware of thoughts as they occur, and We can learn to stay without
them for longer periods.

Now, when We get lost in thoughts, when Our attention is fully drawn
in by the drama and the sense of identity which thoughts give to Us, We
feel them as Emotions that are created within Our body's energy fields.

We experience these sensations of feelings as Emotions, which result
from identification with the thinker. And with the bodily functions, We
feel the sensations of hunger, pain, pleasure, tingling, and sleepiness.

Emotions are sensational Feelings – a mental reflection as a reaction
within the mind/body experience, which comes as the belief in the
illusory thought identity of the perceiver's separate sense of being.

We can feel Emotions as pleasant, comfortable feelings, such as happiness, gratitude, and love, as well as unpleasant, mostly uncomfortable sensations, such as fear, anger, and hate.

"Emotion arises at the place where mind and body meet.
It is the body's reaction to your mind - or you might say,
a reflection of your mind in the body." **Eckhart Tolle**

Emotions can arise without thoughts, but they rarely ever do, and We can't know for sure how it happens. They could be explained as the result of a direct link to Our Souls or that they come from subconscious aspects of the psyche.

We experience & feel Emotions because We identify with the thinking mind. We hold on to the idea of personality, the sense that things are happening to a concept of Me, as a separate point in Time & Space. All these experiences collectively create an ego as an illusory sense of identity. In order to prevent or precede Emotions, We must remain at peace with the inner field of the body, breath, and Consciousness.

We have become experts in evoking Emotions through various activities, arts, and meanings in Life, such as with religion, culture, tradition, race, education, family, friendships, relationships, stories, nationalities, singing, clubs, acting, and every type of affiliation to a particular community or organisation. Above all else, the feeling of Global Healing.

"When a certain number of people come together and they choose
at a moment in time to create a precise emotion in their hearts,
that emotion literally can intentionally influence the very
fields that sustain the life on planet earth." **Gregg Braden**

Emotions are to be entirely accepted & understood, for they are the sensational tool that acts as the extension of the experience of having the mind & body. They help Us differentiate and track thoughts more easily, enabling Us to connect more to Our Soul as the source of Our Living Essence

Mind

Nothing in Existence can be feasibly viewed as an enemy or a threat, let alone something so close to Us as Our own minds. The mind should be seen as a part of creation, the movement of thoughts, and an exciting way to interact with reality, which alone has no associated polarity. The mind & thoughts are simply a relationship of Consciousness' interaction with Existence. We don't need some sort of special science to notice how Our thoughts come & go without pre-empting their occurrence. Our supposed mental involvement with the World gives Us the sense of a corresponding relationship between that which We observe and that which the mind thinks, creating the feeling that We are the Ones who think thoughts. This simple but incorrect observation has been overlooked by the majority of Humans, which has kept Humanity in the servitude of the mind, and in the domain of thinking, for millennia. We have identified with this free-will illusion as the believed authors of Our thoughts. We have essentially settled for mere mind meanderings, thus We'll remain forever perplexed within infinite alleys that the mind can journey to & through. The result is a mind that resembles a never-ending puzzle of endless imagination, based entirely on a false sense of self, inevitably creating a multitude of egos. The consequence is this messy World that We live in. And my God, how it hurts! All the pain & suffering, war, poverty, slavery, hate, racism, violence, hunger, rape, stress, sickness, mistreatment of animals & Nature, domination, killing & fighting, loneliness, abuse of Civilisation through the monetary system & scarcity, and the constant need to involve Ourself in endless drama, a stark contrast with

Consciousness, the unchanging observance that has only one quality, one dimension or state: Unwavering Attention!

In opposition to Consciousness is addiction; any mind/body activity that One can not stop doing voluntarily. The most common forms of addiction are: conversation, food, smoking, drinking, sex, television, video games, social media, money, possessions, power, belonging, and meaning. Addictions are a way of avoiding or indulging in the mind for a short period of time, for which reason they become addictive, as One can never outsmart the mind. The user of substances or pleasures will always have to face the inevitable return to the mind's domain as they create a vicious circle. His ability to focus on the present is overshadowed by a more & more incessant ego and chemical imbalances in the body. Mind & body are an interface with reality, and the ego is the addictive adjustment of them. The easiest & most fundamental way of recognising that We can't be the mind is the apparent fact that We are aware of it. We are Awareness of the mind as well as all other occurrences and perceptions. One should not seek to abolish the mind, rather, only witness its comings & goings. Paradoxically, the person who wants to get rid of the mind is, themself, made up of the mind. Every instance, sense of identity, and ego is a thought-created affirmation. Thus, instead of fighting, arguing, resisting, believing, and suffering the mind, We must stay as the Awareness of it, as in Zen saying : *"If you work on your mind with your mind, how can you avoid an immense confusion?"* By letting it settle, the Self's true identity as mindless Consciousness will dissolve all the confusion and distress of ego. Thus, the mind can only be approached and successfully recognised as the Consciousness that knows it, within which it appears, ultimately from which it is made up.

The mind itself is not a problem but holding on to it is, and We refer to this as ego. The mind is a mental compass in service of Consciousness. With it, We can function & navigate in 3D reality. Like an anchor, it holds us in place, experiencing Existence at this level until it gradually becomes self realised in Consciousness and remains forever known. So the mind is a mirror in the reflections of which We become aware of Ourselves as the Awareness of itself. The ego thrives on the idea of action, drama, doing, and dealing with the World or itself as an object outside of Oneself, therefore terms such as destroying, overcoming, tricking, and fighting the mind may be inviting to it. The ego is a belief in a separate entity. Here it helps to see that We can not deal with such a non-existent entity by giving it the credit of being real at all. We can not deal with the ego. It is enough to do nothing about it to recognise it, to abide as Awareness.

That, however, is extremely difficult for the average Citizen, therefore it is wise to develop practices & techniques for quieting the mind, mindful meditation for example, to gradually open up more space so that Our natural presence of Being can shine unbroken and uninterrupted

Body

The Human Body is the most amazing creation in the Universe!

It Exists so that Consciousness/Spirit/Soul/Mind can have
the final and complete experience of material subtleties.

Yogis mostly sit and do little in Life because there is no mind to
satisfy, and the body doesn't need a lot to survive but a few scraps
of food & water. They surrender and go with the flow of Presence.
When You strip Yourself of all the acts of character, ego, and needs,
the pure Being will remain and there would be no reason or meaning
in doing anything on that base. The only purpose We can talk about
is Self-awareness because, in that state, it is Self-evident. So there
is no point in existing, there is no other reason for Civilisation
other than to become fully conscious and melt back into Source.

If You were truly One with Consciousness, with no separation
between the two, You wouldn't even know You had a Body,
You wouldn't even know You had Yourself. You, as a Soul,
would just exist in the wondrous experience of this
solid matter and fluid energy.

To separate Yourself from that Spirit-Body link,
via ego, is to separate Yourself from God!

Nature still exists in that Original God Form.

Your Body is Your first connection to Life!
While, say, the Soul can exist without a Body,
You have the Body Now, and if You have
something so fundamental to this Life itself,
it means You Are Supposed to Experience it,
Learn Everything & All about it, without the
need to transcend it, for You are One with It.

There is no Body really. You are a Walking Soul!
Your Body is a visible manifestation of
Your Soul's vibrating energy.

To be fully Conscious of Your Soul is to
handle this awesome machine God gave Us.
Every act of ignorance towards the true function
of the Body will result in sickness & discomfort.

Your Body is what You Think, Do, and Eat.
Flood Your Soul Body with Awareness, be
Aware of Yourself. Be Conscious of Every Breath.

Healthy Body, Healthy Mind, and Your Soul, that's the Spirit!

Then, We can do triathlons. We can traverse mountains!
We can Walk & Move Forever. We can Work tirelessly to
Save the Earth and Ourselves. And never get bored again!
Never to lose the grip on this vehicle that We have control of.

Is there anything more Pristine, more Authentic, or more
Natural than moving through Pristine Nature?

Reinvent Yourself by Realising
Your True nature

*   *   *

*I choose to shape this Body to be Fit in Health
while keeping my Mind Open and for Peace
honouring One Sacred Heart filled with Love*

*My Conscious Soul comes from Eternal Light
and Our Life is made in the Image of Blissfulness*

H<u>ealth</u>

There is no such thing as healthy food!

All food is bad for Your health!

Having said that, all natural foods are acceptable, the
real problems start with industrial products & chemicals.

When considering the Human diet today, We are drastically
failing in Our ability to control what should really be serving
Our Health & well-being. We struggle to differentiate real food
from entertainment food, so We unknowingly base Our dietary
options and preferences primarily on unconscious habits.

Most Health issues have direct causes: unhealthy food,
drink, and lack of physical exercise. Stress plays a huge
part too, and in combination with all the junk We eat,
and all the tablets We take, it doesn't help to feel stressed.

We can't blame anybody for this current state; We're all
victims of the system, the marketing, and production. Our
own ignorance is financing these industrial-scale dietary
provisions, which pose a nightmare of temptation for the
indulgence of unconscious taste-yearning mental states.

We should eat with the overall feeling of Our body and
not as a momentary function of satisfying that feeling of
hunger. Diet must be synonymous with Our fitness state.
Food serves Us as an energy fuel but also as medicine and
the building blocks of a Naturally well-functioning body.

Animals in Nature don't have Human problems. Their diet
is as natural as it can be. They don't get fat, skinny, or sick
due to their mental state influencing their dietary preferences.

It has never been easier to Own Yourself, to know what
food is, how the body functions, and how training affects it.
It takes half an hour of exercise every other day to stay in shape.
With that, everything feels better, and it strengthens Our immunity.
The Human body is created for movement, for agility, for endurance;
it takes just a little inspiration and will to keep it functioning & going.

It has also never been easier to fall victim to food & modern-comfort
addictions, which mainly result in laziness and Health issues. So
regular exercise & a Healthy balanced, high-quality, nutritious diet
are a Lifesaver! We can start with juicing, fitness, Inner peace,
and going back to Nature to feel Her nurturing presence.

Still, at the root of Life, it's clear that food oxidises Our
cells, making them age faster and thus shortening
the original length of Human Life on Earth,
which could last for hundreds of years!

We shouldn't eat Living Cells at all,
as Consciousness doesn't need food.
A superfluous, uncentred mind does.

And since Our body is pure energy, We
could sustain Ourselves only by drinking
Water on a Breatharian-Sungazing diet!

This original and mystical way of Life can
only function if the ego is absent, if thoughts
are pure & centred on the issues that matter.

For if We learn and live this knowledge
from a young age, We would, just like
Adam & Eve, walk among Nature
in the perpetual state of

Bliss & Ecstasy

Breath

Look At Your Hands Right Now!
The Human Fist is the most complex and advanced limb in all of Nature!
One which has allowed Us to reshape This Beautiful World.

You can literally control the movements of Your fingers.
You have the Ability to Feel Your Entire Body.
What the Greatest of Gifts This Unique Experience Is!
This Sensation of Being a Living Biological Vehicle,
on the surface of a Planet.
You Are Alive, People! We should Celebrate this Phenomenon
Every Moment, as Each One is the Only One there Is!

But somehow, in building this World, We got used to it because
that's what routine does to You. There are billions of People in the
World, but We feel more isolated & alone than ever. What happened
to make Us so misled, indoctrinated, and misunderstood?

*We got Lost in doing rather than Being. We got Hypnotised by watching
rather than Looking. We got Addicted to pleasure rather than Perception.*

But You're the Greatest Star on the Screen of Consciousness!
Your unique viewpoint matters the most. And We want to
know All about You! So don't be selfish. Follow Your
Creativity and Share Yourself with Ourselves!

See Yourself as a Universal Soul inhabiting the Human
body in this Lifetime. And Feel how it is of little importance
what gender You are or what Your Life situation is.

By being Conscious of Your Awareness,
You transcend the current Human perceptions
and can See the larger framework within which We
all exist, share, and experience Our time on Earth.

You are not Your body, and You are not Your mind.
They are an experience within Awareness.
You already have a victory, why dwell in defeat?
You are New & Lively with each & every Conscious breath!

Like Soul-alchemists of the mind: turn addiction, desire, wanting, and craving into The Middle Way, fear into Life, hatred into Love, worry into Peace, doubt into Courage, sickness into Health, lust into Romance, small-talk into Wisdom, self-pity into The Self, laziness into Strength, war into Deeds, property into Sustainability, poverty into Permaculture, the system into Freedom, the world into Nature, negative into Positive, and leave darkness Dark as it is a natural Light. Return unconsciousness into Consciousness!

"And so, onwards... along a path of wisdom, with a hearty tread, a hearty confidence... however you may be, be your own source of experience. Throw off your discontent about your nature. Forgive yourself your own self. You have it in your power to merge everything you have lived through- false starts, errors, delusions, passions, your loves and your hopes- into your goal, with nothing left over." **Friedrich Nietzsche**

Whenever You have a chance, whenever
You have a moment, Stop, and breathe in deeply.
Give Your mind a break, and breathe in Your surroundings.
Wherever You may be, breathe in the Land, the Sky, the Environment.
Breathe the Country You are in, the Continent, the Earth.
Breathe in The Universe !
Feel as if You are a localised experience of the Entire Existence.

Breathe that Air In, Breathe in those Expanded Horizons,
that New Atmosphere, New Space, and New Time;
Breathe in as the Existence!

That is Who You Are,

Breath

71

CHAPTER 4

ILLUSION

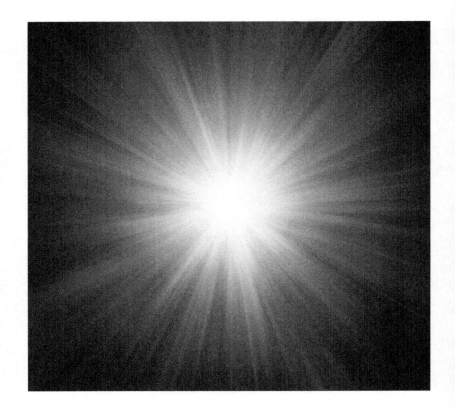

Separation

You think too much, my Dear Human! You think so much that You've
thought Yourself out of Your All-encompassing Oneness with Life.
Or We could say the problem is not that You think too much, rather,
it's that You don't think enough, or even that You don't think at all!

You have created the World of Separation that exists only in Your mind,
which doesn't exist as an independent entity, as all You can observe is
one random thought at a time. *"Thoughts simply appear in Consciousness."*

This apparent independence took You from Knowing to thinking,
but One only Sees the Unity with Being by observing Nature.
There, no individual creature behaves separately from
the Existential Canvas of Divine, Wild Diversity.

*"We are divine beings, not really human beings. The Human comes from
the combination of humus/dirt and the manas/mind. Human is a fallen
state where the mind is identified with the body, with the matter, not
with the supreme light & love, and intelligence of God."* **Shunyamurti**

One must ask then: Why have We forsaken Thee?
> Because We feel separate from that BIGGER picture.
> We feel outside of the Super-unified Field of Source.
> We feel inverted by thinking of Ourselves as isolated.

What brought about this Thinking Separateness?
What is responsible for Humanity existing on its own?
> It's the one System that We created Ourselves, the one
> which began with the mythical Tree of Knowledge.

Why don't tribal people keep eating from the Tree?
> Because They haven't got enough of the wrong fruits.
> Some of Them still Live as One with pristine Nature.
> They Live Connected to the Source and are fully aware of it.

We are Always One with All that IS, with the Being.
But when We do feel separate from It, We are then, by
definition, seeking to return to that Primordial Oneness.

The way We do this is by everything You can see around Us,
everything We've created. All the systems & interactions serve
this sole purpose of giving Us the feeling of not being separate.
I am talking about everything here: relationships, entertainment,
communities, nationalities, universalities, transcendences. All of It.

We often hear how Happiness is Our True nature. Therefore, it is
also a purpose of Life because everything We do is just a means
to make Us happy, whether through money, love, success, or fun.
But happiness is, in fact, only the initial feeling of returning to
the sense of Oneness that was previously lost in Separation.
After a short euphoria, happiness then settles down into Stillness.

"When you lose touch with inner stillness, you lose touch with yourself.
When you lose touch with yourself, you lose yourself in the world."
Eckhart Tolle

Following this, I would obviously state how Peace, or in
the right meaning, Consciousness, is Our True nature!

"Until you make the unconscious conscious, it will
direct your life and you will call it fate." **C. G. Jung**

Hence, The Deeper Purpose Of Life Is To Be Conscious.

And this is the Main Point in the Grand Cosmic Journey of Being!

When You eat enough of the wrong fruits, You are forced to
change Your diet, just as by making the full circle journey in
Self-awareness, You end up Right Back in the Heavenly Garden!
Knowing Your Being, Beyond the thinking mind, in All
of the Existence, as One With All Life, As Pure Beingness

Seclusion

Every moment Someone dies and Someone is born;
every moment Someone experiences suffering or happiness,
sadness or joyfulness; in each moment, We witness miracles of Life.

Can One comprehend the World at LARGE; can One accept the
countless Miracles, like our Earth, which occur every Now throughout
a multiverse of experiences? It is You and I , in Our 'ordinariness,'
that have the privilege of being aware of life's beauty.

The fact that We experience individuality means the viewpoint is
different for everyone. That means We can't seek truth in relation to
equality but in that which is similar to all Conscious beings; pure light
of Consciousness. Then, there is no experience of individuality.

But after a lifetime in ecstasy, We spend an incarnation in agony.

Like that famous philosopher who stayed true to himself by rendering
all kinds of pains of human Seclusion: I am the first decent human being,
he said. What a noblest of the greatest statements this is. Just caring to
be the appreciating Consciousness of Humanity. That is the spirit,
freedom, the will to power, and the courage to live.

Just imagine such dignity of the Self-appointed mastery.
An opening of never seen doors of knowledge,
being on the edge of wisdom, the point of no return to sanity.

He walks in eternity, writes as a self-proclaimed celebrity, knows no
fear, and retires to immortality. And thus, by fulfilling his destiny, while
most of Us walk aimlessly, he became the first decent human being.

With that, his descent from the lonely mountain is ultimately doomed
to failure. *"But whoever is of my kind, cannot escape such an hour, the hour*
which says to him: Only now are you going your way to greatness!"

Man is by nature a lonely soul, a point of Consciousness, never truly
needing anyone but bound to assimilate. If, however, Your love of love
is lesser than Your despising of women, You will join the abyss.

For how could You ever find comfort with the prostitute, compromising
and losing Yourself thus? In this inescapability, We live a life of quiet
desperation. We succumb to the inevitability of seeking happiness,
and aiming for the pointlessness in superficial meanings.

Your values are wrong, Your beliefs artificial, and lack a wider view.
You willingly enter the wheel of karma, the circle of incarnation.
You are lost.

And how can You ever live while being ashamed of Civilisation
by seeing through Their conditioning of ignorance,
only if You are ignorant Yourself?
Now You are tired of new places becoming old;
if One could only ever constantly travel.
You are tired of different women acting the same;
if One could only ever exist and live alone.
I am lost.

Existence is meaningless, and We procreate only to
the degree of unconsciousness - while Consciousness Is!

By calming Our mind through conscious breathing, Awareness
will naturally remain and re-establish itself as the primary identity.
In such an open space, We, as the Conscious Soul, regain the power
of Presence, the freedom to choose based on this sacred intelligence
rooted in timelessness, and therefore will stand the test of time.

Such action is universally recognised as one of no fear
and delivered with compassionate love.

It is the main reason, We feel attracted to
Jesus & Buddha, as They are embodiments of That

Suffering

Everything in the Universe is in Consciousness!
That is the Natural state of Existing.

You Know that by Knowing Yourself, by going
Within and experiencing all the passing perceptions.
You Are that One Truth which is Continuing,
Consciousness, the Underlying Phenomena, The Being!

Self-conscious Beings tend to Forget, to Overlook,
and to Miss Out on Their Essential Nature, which
is thus obscured by the unconscious mind.

There is One basic Law in the Universe:
All things Unnatural will return to their Nature!
Or as Jesus puts it:
Everything in the dark will come to Light.

Just as a balloon can't stay underwater, it requires an outside agency
to keep it under, the ego keep itself submerged within its own identity.
You go around with an image of Yourself, a bundle of thoughts, Your ego,
so most of what happens & plays out in Your Life – action/reaction,
cause & effect scenarios – come from this unconscious part.

It is natural for unconscious Beings to seek the absolute truth of
Themselves by examining an outer World, only to discover the Light
of the Inner Truths, the Consciousness, that is inherent in Them.
This is the base of all religions, philosophies, spiritualities
– and of all the mind & spirit sciences.

You know that there is something strange, unnatural, confusing,
and wrong with the way that Life in this Civilisation functions.
That is the reason You become religious, spiritual, or philosophical,
for it gives You at least some solace throughout Life.

"Have no fear of moving into the unknown.
Simply step out fearlessly knowing that I am with you,
therefore no harm can befall you; all is very, very well.
Do this in complete faith and confidence. Be not afraid!"
Pope Saint John Paul II

Still, You know there is no final Truth or Answer.
So You keep looking & searching for that Unattainable
Knowledge, that Escaping Peace, that Fleeting Bliss.
Or for God, as the Highest Universal Good.

"Even if you are a minority of one, the truth is still the truth."
Mahatma Gandhi

We already examined how Consciousness is the Answer,
the Eternal Truth, which is also the reason You Cannot be truly
happy, forever satisfied, or in lasting Peace. Fully Conscious Life
is impossible, given the circumstances of the World at Large.

This Life is meant to be one of experience,
not one of endless happiness.

As Buddha said: *Life is Suffering.*
Or God's *Divine Dichotomy,*
or The Bible's *Original Sin,*
which is the first rise of ego.

How then, to at least abide in Peace,
or second best, to attain glimpses of Joy?

"Joy knows itself. As children we didn't even know the word joy, we were joy."
Francis Lucille

Whatever arises in mind, observe it without judgment.
Never make a victim out of Yourself.
Never pity Yourself.

By observing these passing states of mind, these
reoccurring thought streams, these unconscious patterns,
recognise the fleeting nature and futility of them.

Surrender in Non-resistance and Acceptance of What Is!

When We dig deep down through the mind, and find the
solid base ground as Awareness, We will, upon looking
back, see through all the temporary manifestations.
We'll see how Our body, gender, personality,
country, Earth, Galaxy, and Universe are constructs
of Our perception, Our egos, and Our unconsciousness.

Meditation helps Us to focus Our attention on Pure Awareness
and relaxes the mind by centring Ourselves as Consciousness.

Re-establish Your mind in that Space, that Openness,
and Focus on Feeling that Freedom in Your Heart.

Discover This Strength in Loving and Peace in Breathing.

Here lies the Power of Being Truly Free, of existing
"In this World but not of It," the End of Duality,
the Source of Unconditional Love,
and possibly Eternal Peace & Joy,
found in Knowing of Your Own Being

*　　*　　*

Through the conundrum of uncertainties & dreams,
We lose Ourselves in the vestiges of an Earthly time.

In the Multiverse of Infinite Possibilities,
You are the Pure Consciousness,
Underlying the Manifestations of an Experiencer

Death

What is Death, and how does it feel to be dead or not alive?

There is no Death really. It is Our temporary body that goes, with Our memories, and dreams. But the foremost ground on which these appear – Consciousness – is ever-present. It never dies.

You already have the experience of how it feels to be without such experiences, every night during sleep. Sleep is how it feels to be Dead, so to speak, as You remember nothing.

Your mind is at such peace during sleep that thoughts don't arise, and since it doesn't dream, there is nothing in which Consciousness can recognise Itself; there is only Pure Awareness present, and that feels like Nothing, like the absence of memory, like not existing, like not remembering. It simply feels like Being. It is like being Dead.

So Death feels like Eternity in the moment, which is what Consciousness Is. But don't worry, You won't remember it!

"At times, I almost dream. I, too, have spent a life the sages' way and tread once more familiar paths. Perchance I perished in an arrogant self-reliance an age ago... and in that act, a prayer for one more chance went up so earnest, so... instinct with better light let in by death that life was blotted out not so completely... but scattered wrecks enough of it to remain dim memories... as now... when seems once more... the goal in sight." **The X-Files,** The Field Where I Died

If Our identity survives the physical Death, it will adapt itself to its Soul essence, giving it inevitable newfound freedom from the body & mind.

Identity means holding on to any idea of Self and The World.

If You're scared of Death, You are probably afraid of the physical pain, which is often the case in those last moments of having the Conscious experience of bodily sensations. Or You're simply fearful of not existing, for maybe You love Life so much that it makes You afraid of losing it.

Mark Twain delivers a perfect description of the above point:
Death, I do not fear death. I've been dead for billions of years before I was born, and had not suffered the slightest inconvenience from it.

Another taste is given in Gandalf's statement:
I have no memory of this place, and
every day was as long as the life age of the Earth.

These thoughts of non-existence are the only place where fear exists. For this reason, it is said that every fear is the fear of dying. But what is there to be afraid of? Death is simply Nothingness, and Life is the experience of Somethingness. The experience of thoughts, feelings, sensations, and perceptions, all present, bundled, and appearing within Our minds, where We can access old thoughts, which We call memories.

Death or Eternal Sleep is like not remembering anything, but it's not the absence of Consciousness or Awareness; it is *The Awareness of Absence,* as **Rupert Spira** points out.

Everything is always an experience in Consciousness. And the experience of Consciousness that has no current experience is exactly how it feels when We sleep or We are Dead, which is simply when Consciousness is 'sleeping' Itself.

There is no Death as such, for Consciousness is always Here. There is Only an Experience of the Absence of Experience!

That is The Eternal Life, and it's the Best feeling ever. It's the Only feeling ever – the Most freeing feeling!

It is Just Nothing, Just Dark,
of The Eternal LIFE

Birth of Love

You've been dreaming again, waking up the passion!
Are We the same Soul having different experiences? Maybe We've
been together in previous lives, or We're preparing for the next one?
Shall I tame You with a Cupid's arrow or leave it be? You have to know
I still find dreams about You, Us, and Our alternative free ways of Life!
Where again, We've connected so deeply in Love that it beggars belief
but borders believable, as it feels more of a dream than a possible reality.
But We can finally make some sense of this newfound tenacity in Our
freed hearts, who, although are slaves to this Love, yes, are drawing
such strength from it that Ours feel as liberated as any Soul could be.
I bow to You in reverence, holding my pride hostage for Your
beautiful being and Your beating loving heart. I have Loved You in
the ways nobody else ever did. I've looked at the Universe in Your eyes,
talked to Your Soul infinitely while touching Your lips softly with mine,
which seemed like an eternity to wait to feel... gentle, sweet, and
warm, like only Gods would dare to imagine and care to perform!
So blessed, We have made the most private Love between Us, where
We truly became One in a hug of loving hearts, holding hands,
playing, and smiling in each other's palms! I've been the essential
deity to You, in every moment of Our Life, as You deserved me to
be, for You are my devotee, and We both desire that which can
flee! For as the famous poet Rumi said: *"True lovers never meet!"*
I will always stay as God to You – imagine me heavenly, and
You will always be forbidden fruit for me – I keep dreaming
of You heartedly because We are never meant to be, even if We
have always been here. If You are ready and feel safe, I will go
back to my Universal existence and You to Your Worldly ways,
where We preserve this divine idea and inspire each other as
long as We stay true to Ourselves We'll thus, stay true, to that
which indeed is so rare! I hope, in Your Life now, You have all
the Love in the World, as I have all the Love of Your World.
*I like to play with words to create worlds and destinies, just as
somebody, somewhere, is now dreaming & creating this One*

Ephemera of Dreams

When You sleep & dream, You're creating an entire experience of
Life with Your thoughts. You are imagining, that is, dreaming,
a World as convincing as This One Is. In fact, Our dreams
look & feel so real that We believe them. It is only when We
wake up that they reveal themselves to Us as dreams.

There is no scientific evidence to suggest a difference
between the two, between Our real Life and dreams, and
only the degree of length and quality of the dreams makes Us
differentiate them. And actually, the dream world is truer and
more real to who Your subconscious is, for those dreams are
a reflection of the lack of experiences in the Waking World.

You are dreaming random imaginings of fears and desires to
catch up with the experiences You want – but You're running
away from. So listen to Your dreams as they're telling You what
You're missing out on in Life! Dreams are, therefore, an attempt
by Your mind to get what it needs to stay in tune with Life.
Dreams are also a way of Our Soul inspiring Us to address Our
unconsciousness, as We start losing Ourselves in the World.

Dreams are a by-product of the way We live within Civilisation.

Tribal people have no dreams. They focus more on visions and other
altered states of mind to understand This Life. And You're dreaming
because Your Life is not in alignment with Your Soul. Life is a Dream of
the Soul, and Sleep is when Our Soul is resting, so We shouldn't even
have dreams. We should be in complete peace & rest during sleep.

But most people have dreams caused by unfulfilled desires.
Buddha said that all desire is suffering, so then imagine
what unfulfilled desire is doing to Our Humanity?
And Osho said, *"Dreams are your Unlived Life."*

We live in a World of incredible suppression, lack, and suffering. This unfulfilled Life creates tremendous pressure and is the cause of most mental problems and crimes. There is an extraordinary level of discomfort going on in the World.

That is why psychiatrists & healers are interested in Your dreams, for the content of Your dreams gives Them clues to understand Your daily Life and the way You live it.

If We want to make The World more comfortable to live in, We need to address these dream issues.

The easiest way of returning to Our Inner peace and staying more focused on Our current experience, rather than fantasising and dreaming dreams, is to orient All Our Attention towards this constant quality of Being: the Conscious Breath.

Since every Human has the same Consciousness, regardless of different levels & states of the Souls, Consciousness is always the same in Everyone. It's like Air and We are It. There is nothing else, nothing outside of it, other than this Knowing of Being Aware.

You can feel it Right Now by sitting still, relaxed, and as You let go of stress, feel the pressure on Your forehead, the third eye. That is the force of Pure Consciousness expressed through the body as sensation. It is this Pure Presence that is the entry point to Our Freedom, Peace & Love.

And You shouldn't just believe this.
Experience it, and Live it as Reality.

Listen to the needs of Your Soul.
Never dream again.
Live
Your
Dreams

Shores of Playfulness

Amidst Oceans in Our eyes, blissful tears reflect the flickering
vastness of the horizon's shine, which is there like a mirroring
atmosphere of clearest Prussian blue and turquoise-green Seas.

These tranquil waves of wisdom, enduring love, and fortune
are turning into stormy waters by but a shadow of a doubt,
as Your serene, shameful peace overshadows You now.
You're blindly following thoughts about situations that
aren't even there, as if lost in the morning Sea mist,
swimming in the waters of disbelief, against the current,
going against the wind, as You've been cast away on an
open Ocean, and once more You are floating alone, facing
the most frightening scenario to have ever confronted
Man – even scarier than the fear of public speaking.

That epic fear arises with the sharks as panic attacks, the
Moby Dick of lies, with killer whales, and monsters of the
deep, a melancholy that You want to keep, to finally being
saved on a Desert Island that is reminiscent of Your suicidal
tendencies, chronic depression, and deprived isolation.

Now You have been awakened in lucid dreams in the Lost
World of pristine never-yet-seen beaches, covered with: a tapestry
of shelves, glittering mesmerising oyster pearls, shallows overgrown
with coral reefs of unimaginable beauty, crystallised salt formations,
marine-rich life exhibiting an entire array of colours, camouflaged
octopuses, fluorescent medusas resembling the Crab nebula, clouds of
ray fish looking like invading aliens and underwater spaceship fleets.
Oh, what a sight to see! And on the land, vertical bamboo structures,
sky-soaring fresh waterfalls & cliffs, lifesaving lush green forests &
streams. These days are of an endless Sun, clear night skies
with a million shimmering far-reaching lights of Stars,
inducing the Heart talk of the liberated Soul.

This Natural serenity is in You, reclaiming childhood feelings of
freedom, as smooth as the drifting sand under Your barefoot
steps, overpassing clouds move swiftly as if painted solid.
And palm trees below hang on the whitewashed shores
where You've written in hope the 'Help Me S.O.S.' note,
because You're tired of screaming alone like an extinct Dodo
bird when, in truth, You want to be a caring, friendly dolphin.

For the hopeless boredom waiting for help, name me the
One Book You would take on this lonely Isle of despair.
It is This book of an Awakened Heart that will transform the
isolation into an savouring Oasis. So much so that this tropical
paradise no longer reflects in You a wish for suicide. Instead,
it invites overflowing Joy on forgotten Shores of Playfulness,
that is Now a welcoming home, after realising that a Wilson of
the mind is finally gone, or, it that was never there to begin with.
It was just a mind trick – an **ILLUSORY** manifestation – born from
the lack of communication among the close-to-You loved Ones
and Your incrementally reducing collaboration
with the vast World of fellow Humans.

Now, the holy, refreshing coconut water
quenches the thirsty Soul, meaty mango fruit feeds
the starving body, and the raw, nourishing Seaweed
fulfills the lacking brain, recovering and healing You
from the high fever of tropical mind-storms and
rain showers of Your tender, tear-saturated cheeks,
the long-abandoned but, to You, destined dreams,
manifested as nightmares, as Fata Morgana
on the Seas, tsunamis, hurricanes, and earthquakes
of the stress-shaken and weakened immune system.
But acquiring those vital minerals and crucial vitamins
in the form of nutritious and Self-sufficient photon
rays of Illuminating Light Awakens in You

the True Purpose of a Happy Life

Depression

*Depression means being bored with the old as the
feeling arises that something new needs to come into Life.*

It is the overflow of regrets & remorse – a surplus of dwelling
and overthinking. It is being resistant to Your True Self, a belief in
separation, a deep fear of being alone, being without inspiration,
and ultimately the fear of death.
We can change that addiction to feeling sorry for Oneself
via a simple shift towards a Positive Attitude in Life,
that's free from personal judgment, but also embraces Our
uniqueness through the Courage of Expressing Ourselves.

Embrace the current situation and see it clearly as a product of
all previous interactions. Commit to work on healing & progress
daily & hourly. Don't leave space for pity or boredom. Set Your
ideas straight and break them into manageable daily, weekly,
monthly and yearly goals. This vision, this plan of doing
and executing, is the organiser of Our Life's progress.

We measure Achievement in the straightforwardness of momentary tasks.

To go the distance, We must improve Our diet, strengthen Our bodies,
and clarify Our mental focus and determination by experiencing the
benefits of such a wellbeing approach on a moment-to-moment basis.

*"Depression is becoming a pandemic; its origins are complex, from
pathology to negative lifestyles. A culture of prevention is vital."* **Sadhguru**

Breaking the inescapable circle of Depression, which can invoke
suicide, comes down to fulfilling Our true purpose within society.
This means acting on the highest joy, expressing the deepest selves,
creating from an original insight, tracing back to the source of
sorrow, and transcending the old by allowing the New

Ego

The Fact that an Individual Person, a separate point in Time & Space,
can become Aware of Itself, is the Most Intriguing Phenomenon!

This Ability, this Happening, this Self-control,
when You can step outside of the stream of thoughts,
and be One with the Looking Itself, with Conscious Gaze,
and even furthermore to drop the Sense of Self, and Abide
as Beingness, having no Outside or Inside Influence,
to Be One with the Present, as the Self-awareness,
is the High Point of Evolution – Consciousness!

Being Conscious means nothing supernatural,
extraordinary, mystical, religious, intelligent,
better or worse than anything or anyone else.
It means You're not identifying with a thinker,
with the current thoughts, and You no longer
draw a sense of Self from whatever is perceived.

This also means that You are no longer a victim or
subject of Your unconscious mind, of feelings, thoughts,
instincts, urges, desires, and all other ranges of perpetual
needs, which creates this idea of Self through satisfying
that unconscious entity, that artificial construct We've
indoctrinated & inherited from the World at large,
through Our upbringing in its present-day
and age, that entity We call the Ego.

Ego is a Belief in the Separate Self.
The feeling that You are a Mindful Individual.
The Sense of Need to continually add something to
You in order to Fill-in the Ever-present feel of Miss & Lack.

And all the World's problems have arisen from this area of confusion.

*"Everything is interconnected, and the biggest secret of all, to me,
is the extent to which individuality is an illusion."* **David Wilcock**

Ego implies identification with various games and forms, such
as nationality, culture, faith, politics, gender, personal stories, and
relationships, etc., which are all merely flavours of manifestations.
Conversely, deeper Truth is a knowing field where all these
facets of Selves are playing on Life's movie screen.

And since You can't have a Movie without a Screen,
You can't have an experience without Consciousness.
Whether You are aware or unaware during the experience,
Consciousness is always there; it is the only existing quality.
Everything else is dreamed, imagined, played out through
thought or form, philosophised, reasoned, argued,
forced, altered, urged, added to, or taken from.
But Consciousness is the only continuous stream.
And Ego is a feeling of being threatened.

In retrospect, ask Yourself: Am I Safe in this moment?
Is there any apparent danger to my existence, Right Now?
Or do We imagine all problems but can fix them by applying the right
actions, doing what We should do to sustain Ourselves physically?
Is there any real threat other than that of physical survival?

Ask Yourself, is everything else not just a figment of imagination?
Of news, public opinion, of the local or global Status Quo?

*"There can only be one solution to any problem:
a change in attitude and in consciousness."* **Gregg Braden**

In truth, there are No Problems! You are safe & fine just as You Are.
And even if You have unconscious or Ego traits, these still do not
underlie the basic truth, which is being in the present moment, and
doing what You're doing with focus & determination, to succeed right
now, having no flaw or opinion of the task currently experienced.

The task neither asks for Your opinion,
about how You feel nor about what You think.
It has to be completed for Life to continue.

Hence, a demonstration of Responsibility is
the Ability to Respond to the Task Ahead!

When We flow with the general necessities of Life, and
act from that Responsibility State rather than from Ego,
it is like being thrown into the Freedom of doing exactly
what needs to be done, without adding any extra effort.

Then, We complete tasks in a single moment of utmost
dedication, without thoughts in mind, without stepping out
of the stream of inspiration that flows without the hindrance
of procrastination, engaging only with the present action.

It is through such openness that synchronicity can play a major
role in Our Lives since We're aligning Ourselves with the natural
flows of interaction, better known as The Law of Attraction!

*"Your purpose is to be YOU as fully as you can, and the way
that's perhaps most easily done is to act on your highest joy."*
Bashar/Darryl Anka

When the Ego is absent, Creativity Flows In like
an open art book, with no resistance, with a Love of the
Human Soul, which then actualises in manifestations of the
innermost talent to express a Beauty that Life in Love Is.

We All have these same innate abilities to Live the Life
of Our Dreams. We are All the same Spark of Light.

*As We Act on these Newfound Revelations, We are Influencing
the World's Transformation, which will Echo across the Universe,
as Love from Our Souls' Reverberations*

Who Are We

Who Are You? What makes a person the Person?
What gives a person Their Character and Behavioural Traits?

If You were born in Ancient Rome, You would be
a Roman, unaware of these Future times, and
You would only know what was known then.

You wouldn't be You, as You are Now.
So that which makes You You
is the Time & Culture You are born into.

If You want to know how it feels to be Chinese,
meet a Chinese person or move to China and completely
integrate into Their society. With that, upon experiencing the
essence of Their culture, You will start to become Chinese.

Everybody in the World is just another You, experiencing
a particular set of mainly localised influences.

If You can be moulded into any personality depending on Your
circumstances, it follows that it's Your mind which is adjusting.

But the One & Only experience which Never Changes
is the Same and Ever-present Witness.

That Which Is Witnessed Always Changes
and Never Stays The Same!
It Is Witnessing That Always Remains!

Therefore, You are nothing external, nothing that is under
the conditions of outside influences. You're essentially only
the platform upon which Your persona is developing, and
that Platform, that Space of Aliveness, is Consciousness.

Understanding This gives You Peace.

"Peace is not something you wish for; It's something you make, something you do, something you are, and something you give away." **John Lennon**

The constant search for happiness is a by-product of the inability to See and Recognise Yourself as Awareness, to See a Fleeting Nature of All Experience.

If You are still the subject and victim of cultural surroundings & styles, and if You still identify with any idea, basing Your existential sense on it, then You are, by definition, not yet Self-aware.

In Self-awareness lies the recognition of the diminishing nature of all forms & ideas, and therein lies the Conscious freedom of drawing no sense of Self from such temporary mind creations.

Self-Awareness Is an Evolutionary Pulse of the Ability to Self-reflect!

If You are aware of Your thoughts and See how they appear without order or pre-knowledge of them, You can remain as that Awareness, always prior to the occurrence of any thoughts & feelings. You are then a Witness of Your mind and not a victim of it. As You realise this mental habit entirely, You will subsequently step outside of that domain of thoughts, where, instead of You, there is Pure Consciousness Experiencing Itself Remaining.

When We were kids, We didn't have a true ego; We were not fully aware either, but fascinated, since everything just happened as a sequence of habits, instincts, urges, and external causes. As We learn a language, believing that idea of Self, compared with and separate from Others, ego is created, as well as increased Awareness, which stays covered by the ego for as long as the illusion and mass mentality influence Us, that is, provided We don't Awaken enough Self-awareness to completely break through the mind-dominated Self.

This Freedom from Yourself is able to happen in each moment by staying fully Present; this allows for a Continuous uninterrupted state of Clear, Thoughtless, Egoless Looking-out.

In other words, it is the Conscious Self-awareness. Consciousness is going to the base of the experience. It's the very knowing by which experience is known. So to Know Who We Are, We must apply the same search for the origin and real experiential Truth in every experience, in every term, behind every meaning.

If We consider LOVE, it can only mean Oneness.
It is a recognition of Our True nature as a Human collective.
It is a constant honouring of the Humanity in Everyone.
It is the Equality of the Global Community, as a Universal Family.

Love results from the melting of Our egos, revealing a natural presence of appreciation for all Beings, for All of Life.

"Infinite Love is the Only Truth - Everything Else is Illusion"
David Icke

Love is synonymous with Consciousness; they are ONE.
Love is not a feeling or an attribute We seek outside,
but it is Being Free within Conscious experience.
Love is the Life of God, the Life of Our Souls.
It is Consciousness' recognition of Itself.

This Life is the Evolution of Self-awareness in Love.
As the mantra of **Ram Dass** goes, *"I AM LOVING AWARENESS!"*

It then becomes Self-evident to such a degree that this Self-witnessing Occurrence needs to happen. Yes, it is Civilisation vs. the Snake, if You will, the snake who gave Us an Apple and an ego. And it is Our Destiny
to Take Back
Control of Ourselves

Know Everything

Looking at any Ant colony, We can see a particular hierarchical set of naturally inherited behaviours. We could leave the ants alone forever and they'll live the same way indefinitely, should circumstances stay the same. But it is not the same with Humans.

We, Humans, have the capacity to learn, change, and evolve. We have the ability to progress from apparently simple worker Ants, to a supervisor, to a manager, to the director, to being Queen.

Above all, We have the unique capacity to transcend the entire chain of the game, the monopoly, the system. The entirety of the Civilised experience.

My fellow Humans, We have the Ability to Transcend Existence!

How Do You Do This? You do this by Knowing Everything !

For it is not only possible to Know Everything, It Is Absolutely Mandatory For You To Do So!

Of course, I don't mean knowing every book, piece of information, or learning every detail, for that is just having a great memory. It is not even about being smart or intelligent, for that is just being clever within the confines of Your mind.

Intelligence is not the measure of Wisdom, The Knowing Is!

What I mean by Knowing Everything is to UNDERSTAND the Underlying Principles according to which We Exist, Create, and Evolve!

The Beginning of Understanding is the End of ignorance!

"By 'known,' I meant understood." David Deutsch

When You Understand how Consciousness is fundamental to all of Existence, including You, You know You are It. Therefore, there is no You. It is only Consciousness, Presence, Observance, Knowing. And because of this Knowing, there are no other answers to be given since there are no further questions left to be asked.

"Don't try to understand! It's enough if you do not misunderstand."
Nisargadatta Maharaj

We could ask an infinite number of questions regarding Existence, all the details of its laws & manifestations, the relationship between subjects & objects, and the intricacies of Our perceptual experiences.

But all of those are merely extrapolations from One's Awareness. The Human mind, Science, and philosophy of any branch involve answering all the questions, but the Final Spirituality gives only One answer, since they are all experienced in Consciousness:

It is to Know Yourself! To Know Thyself!

It is to be fully Conscious of Yourself!
It's to melt into the Existential Canvas
upon which all experiences happen.

It is to stand outside any experience and,
with that, to See & Understand the general & driving
force behind the Creation, behind any & every Existence.

It is to observe how ants behave, how animals behave,
how Humans behave, how Aliens, and even God behave!

It is to be free from Your mind, and within that expanded
Awareness, to be fully aware of every Atom in Existence,
as there is only the single One, which is of Your making.

It is to fully immerse Yourself in Consciousness

CHAPTER 5

TRAVELLING

Travel

Travel is synonymous with Spirituality,
History, and Art! It is the on-the-spot recognition and
example of Our shared being. It is Spirituality in motion.

Consciousness is then the best companion during travelling,
for it makes You See everything in a free, general, and open way.

When You orientate Yourself to the artistic aspect of creation,
acknowledging all the love, time, will, inspiration, soul, design,
and talent that went into bringing any art-form into Life,
You will thus cherish all works of art, no matter what religion,
style, culture, tradition, or idea they belong to and represent,
for it is all a wonderful expression of the Human Soul.
Creation is the Driving Force of Existence!

Imagine how much Alien art there is in the entirety of Existence.
There must be an infinite number of Civilisations, creations, designs,
colours, and shapes. By being conscious of the possibilities of
options in creating, You're non-judgmentally allowing
the observance, acceptance, and witnessing of
billions of different kinds of forms.

That's what the Universe is – a Play, an Art-form!

To Travel is to Feel Exhilaration with such Energy. It is to
feel that Sacred Cultural Enrichment deepen Your Intellect & Heart,
the very Soul. The Very Atmosphere which makes the World a Magical
Dream of Sites and Scenes, of beautiful Architectural Splendour.

The Dream We all need to appreciate and cherish. Not only in its
Monuments and Buildings but in its People. Because Our People are
the Ones to pass on Our History, Traditions, and all those Great
Classical values for generations yet to come!

Restore Your Institutions and Your Churches, Preserve old Streets and Squares, Honour Your Worldly Heritage my Brothers and Sisters!

Imagine all the squares, parks, museums, churches, and vistas. The World of street musicians, tourist lines, historically precious ruins, and religiously magnificent structures.

This gives You an Understanding of the Real World in art, brick and stone. It Teaches You to appreciate and cherish All Diversities of Nations, Regions, People, and Traditions.

This Sensation of Valour Elevates Our Spirit to yet Uncharted Areas of Perception Previously Unexplored by the Unconscious masses. But Forever Edged and Skilfully Carved in Eternity, Dating back from Universal Scale Epoch to Prehuman Age, through Classical Eras, Imperial Empires and Aristocracy, through Monarchy, and Democracy to Modern Times.

Travel is an intellectually valuable Déjà vu experience. It is larger than Life because it shapes Lives.

It is a method of reliving everything You knew, but this time in a close, real & personal way, and a whole lot more.

Travel is a movement of both Past & Future, equally entertained in Your mind's eye, of History and an entire World of Art. It's this Journey of Your Spirit that Dances in Your Mind, Envelops Your Heart, Moves Your Soul.

For The Love of God, You don't travel, It Travels YOU

*   *   *

I AM Ancient and Now

Romantic Aspiration

Once You taste the enjoyment of being an Independent researcher, You'll know that the Best Knowledge You will ever have is Personal Experience.

So the best thing about it is gaining such knowledge first-hand.
This makes learning that much more exciting and fun, as
opposed to sitting in some classroom and memorising
information that doesn't hold immediate importance.

For these simple, obvious, and fun facts of Life,
moving, seeing, understanding, and comprehending
the Historical & Cultural World around Us is a Must.
This means that museums and churches, together
with architectural and historical treasures,
are the most important heritage in Life!

Without the knowledge of Ourselves, of Why and for
Who are We living, or of what is actually worth caring for,
Who are We if We don't know these Truths?

"It is only with the heart that one can see rightly; what is essential is invisible to the eye." **Antoine de Saint-Exupéry,** The Little Prince

Literate depth is the greatest Soul gift One can render, as it can
be used to enrich Humanity. Thus, We've embedded all these
details of Knowledge of Life within Culture & Art as Soul Values.
And together with the natural healing environment,
it gives Us a True sense of the Human Self.

Following this, the most Romantic Aspiration that a Human can have
is to Dream of Ancient Civilisations, The Meaning, the Mesmerising
Mystery. To be a Historian, Scientist, Archaeologist, Culturologist,
Egyptologist, Palaeontologist, Biologist, Geologist, Botanist, Chemist,
Linguist, Teacher, Researcher, Author, or an Ancient Astronaut.

Humanity has provided Us numerous different types of Civilisation, Art, Architecture, Culture, Faith and Knowledge, as well as Feelings. We are the Continuation of Humans' Efforts at Living.

We Owe Them!

Regardless of whether God or an Architect Created or Simulated the Universe, or whether it's here just by Itself, We already know virtually everything about The Nature of this World that They, The Ancients, Dreamed about knowing.

For a long time, They thought Everything was made of Earth, Air, Fire, and Water.

But We played with Chemistry, separated all the compounds into their constituent parts, and found the Building Blocks of Matter – the Fabric of Reality. We Know it is made out of 92 naturally occurring Elements.

We went even deeper and found Atomic & Subatomic particles, so much so that, We even created new Elements. We literally played with Creation.

We Constructed an Entire World out of weird & artificial New materials & substances.

We also played with Biology and Genetics – We played God!

It's Obvious.
We Are completing the Full Circle of Life.
Perhaps Future Generations will read about Us in History books, or some Universal record, as extinct, evolved, or good, New & Alive
As Us

Time

The further back in History & Time You go,
the more authentic the experience of the Culture becomes!

This is why historic buildings & ruins with tradition, works of art, books & artifacts are the most valuable records of the Past that We have. Authentic infrastructure and iconic buildings are an important expression of original inspiration of style & art. This is what We call classical, simply the apparent natural progression of architecture, with examples being Pyramids & Greek temples. But it still takes insight & daring to create something new, even if it feels natural. When something becomes a habit, then We call it a style.

History is a Living Legend, and to Travel in the
search for One is the Real-Life Documentary!

Imagine the World hundreds of years ago, without the internet, TV, newspapers, telephones, radios, or even books. There was only infrastructural originality, tales, and stories.

It was not a Black & White World; it Never was.
It was as Real & Surreal as it will Ever be!
To get glimpses of It makes You weep from Joy,
and rejoice in the Presence of the Past!

Alternating between these New & Old Worlds daily
certifies You as a Time Traveller indeed.
And off Your Spirit goes

*   *   *

It is in each Moment of Eternity that History unfolds Itself.
And on the Timeless place of Ancient stone, I relive it

In Space

Space, Time, Consciousness !

Why do We invest in the Space Race? Why are
We so obsessed with the Exploration of Space?

Because the Technological progress of Humanity
is the driving force of Our Civilisation, and
Space is the Foremost & Final Frontier!

To fantasise about the Universe is the Traveller's Ultimate Dream!

As in the Spirit of the Ancient Mariners, that endless Sea of Space
is the Great Unknown. Reaching for that which is beyond is the
greatest Human passion, as is the Zest for Knowledge, Zeal for
the Truth, and for Understanding of Universal Music. Lucky Us!

This Marching Beat, Rhythm of the Stars, and Melody of a vast,
distant Spatial Silence remind me of the French colonial
Legionnaires' march through the Sahara while being overwhelmed
by exotic animals and people of colour in strange clothing. They saw
mirages shaping in the distance, for there, the sand was burning.

That exploratory Tune remind me of the glorious expedition days,
that original drive to discover and explore faraway lands. The Time
when You couldn't fake the distance, and a Time when the World was
as real as it ever could be. This was when explorers, missionaries and
colonists for the first time saw camels, giraffes, monkeys, and tigers;
when They, for the first time, saw the World outside of Their own.

It reminds me of Alexander the Great's unprecedented drive
to conquer the East, where He met mighty Indian elephants.
His goal & vision? To reach the End of the World and be
the first to put the entire World under One Roof.

This Voyager's Tune reminds me of the Time when explorers broke new boundaries and pushed Humanity forwards by discovering unknown lands, bridging cultures, and uniting traditions.

It's the Time of Roman Legions marching across the unknown Ancient World, with the Glorious Idea of making it known, creating One Civilised Empire, essentially wanting to have all the spices in one cart, under one toga, ready to go!

All of this You can imagine & feel when You close Your eyes and let this Cosmic Music speaks for itself. Let this Space-Bolero by Ravel unravel from the same source it entered the divine composer's stream of imagination.

If You can Think and Feel something, this very Act of Imagination makes it Real, regardless of whether it happened, or if it can or cannot happen. Your power of Conscious recognition is All that ever matters.

Stories, movies, and songs are worth the same or even more than the actual events. It is all the same to Your Mind, Heart, and Soul.

"When you want something with all your heart,
that's when you are closest to the Soul of the World.
It's always a positive force." **Paulo Coelho**, The Alchemist

So this was the Time when people who had travelled came back after many years on the Go. They came back with Stories too unbelievable to accept, and yet We took them as Our Own, because that which They spoke of awakened something essentially Human in All of Us.
It Awakened, Our SOUL

*　　*　　*

"As a traveler, I've often found that the more a culture
differs from my own, the more I am struck by
its essential humanity." **Rick Steves**

City

Every town has its Origins, History, and Soul. It is where most
of Humanity's action happens – a vast global playground.
To navigate the ever-changing city grid is a voyage of endless curiosity &
discovery. It is when One explores & observes a city without prejudice &
judgment that true magic awakens. When You get that Feel for someone
else's reality, oftentimes better than Yours.

If You love Your City, well, everybody else loves Their cities too!
Travelling & photography is a way of experiencing & understanding such
love in every existential sense. It is the exploration of endless possibilities
of creating and rearranging the World, and mostly it is seeking those
cultural values that make Us Human.

It's when You allow Yourself to melt into the streets that You
fall in Love with the culture, buildings, and energy of the
never-ending stream of people, who bring the city to Life in
so many characteristic ways, wherever it is You go in the World.

And to know the World, You have to know the Continents & Seas.
To know the Continents, You have to know the Countries & the Land.
To know the Countries, You have to know their Cities & Villages.
To Understand the City is to know the World.
And Travelling is the biggest game in the World!
It is The World itself. An Ultimate Religion and Revival of the Soul.

In this game of Tradition, a Church is the most beautiful
structure ever conceived. A True Oasis of the Sacred Heart!
And what You carry in Your Heart is all that ever matters.

So knowing Where, Why, and How Humanity Is,
Is the Unification in the Art of Being Human!
It brings out the primary drives: Love, Peace, Joy, Aliveness.

This type of Openness in Travel and in Life is who We are, in many
different shapes & forms, represented by expressions of Our Will to Live.

Travel is going back to Source, starting and
restarting, again & again, every time!
It is to be Born and to Die continuously.
To be Overwhelmed by Arriving and
be Heartbroken by Departing,
and by everything, I mean Every Thing:

The history, culture, architecture & infrastructure.
The ancient city core, or inviting modern centre.
The location and climate, rivers and hills, Nature.
The stories, streets, Cathedrals, museums, art & temples.
The authentic products, music, shows, food & cuisine.
The tourists and the empty alleys, liveability.
The meaning and feeling, romance and memories.
Those Iconic postcards in front of larger-than-Life structures.
The Nation, the Region, the Community, THE NATIVE PEOPLE.
The very Life of LIFE of the place of the City!

It's a Soul's Way of Life – a tasteful Journey in Knowledge.
An Adventurous Dream!
Widening of the Mind and Glorification of the Spirit.

Everything else is Waiting,

"To Travel is to Live"

*   *   *

Well Met Medieval Traveller!

As You Stand upon this Hallowed Ground,
Echoing Ancient Songs, Feudal Wars, Myth & Legend,
Honour a Glorious Age where Chivalry & Knights
Re-enter the Time of
MAGNIFICENT CHURCH BUILDERS

Church

The Church is a Religious Museum, A Spiritual Sanctuary,
The House of GOD!

I have never seen two identical Churches and only very few
that are similar indicating a unique and authentic style of
Infrastructure, or what I would call ARTiTECTURE.

Our World is synonymous with Ancient History, as
We preserve Our Tradition, Our Heritage, Our Sacred Past,
the Holy Present, and the Revelations of the Future.

Thus, We have created & saved the most magnificent architectural
Human achievements, in the form of Cathedrals, Basilicas,
and Churches, with many of them being priceless.

Priceless as Cultural Foundations,
Artistic Masterpieces, and Faithful Fountains!

The Church is a Marvellous Site, an Evolving Stone Edifice!

It is History's favourite building – a place for prayer,
contemplation, meditation, worship, singing, and learning.

No matter which God You are praying or devoted to,
what matters is what awakens inside: Peace, Love, or Blessing.

Every Faith is Based upon The Core Truth of Life, and this
knowledge is one reason for the need to institutionalise it as a
Religion, to protect & pass it down to the next generations.

All religions are a beautiful expression of that core need
for a higher and transcendental purpose to Life, to God.
All are filled with authentic, priceless arts.

Yes, religion is also a reason to fight and die, since its
identity is interwoven with Life itself. It transcends
body & mind. It is, therefore, one of those
Essence Ideals that is larger than Life.

This Mysterious and Otherworldly Feeling,
which Emanates from the Soul Essence of Faith,
Sparked those Visions that lead the Architects
to go to such impressive lengths, giving rise to
the Most Awe-Inspiring Structures on Earth!

This Otherworldly Feeling is thus manifested in the
splendour of Gothic Cathedrals, whose Imposing Spires
allow for the city's best views. And as Flowering
Windows, Flying Buttresses, the Rich Colourful
Decor of Renaissance and Baroque times.

It then implies Beyond Comprehension or
Realisation that such Structures even Exist.

And they will remain Eternally Engaging,
as a Photographer's Paradise, and
a Tourist's Heaven,

Mana of the Spirit
and

Bliss for Our Soul

*   *   *

*"All the darkness in the world
cannot extinguish the light
of a single candle."*
St. Francis of Assisi

Forevermore

You know!
We have been here many times.
You & I. We've done this for so long,
as long as You remember, You & Me.

When days seem endless and repeating
when Life feels like a Groundhog Day. Then,
You'll know in the mind's Déjà vu moments
that the fact You exist Right Now, against all
other playful possibilities of realities, is the
most cherishing experience We could have.
We!

And maybe You'll know this on Your deathbed,
or We'll know this at the moment of Our Rebirth.
But I'm certain, one way or another, sooner
or later, when no time is wrong,
You'll Remember Me,
as I Remember You,
Again and Anew,

That We are Here Forever after,
As We have been here,

Forevermore

*   *   *

*I'm mesmerised by those Déjà vu moments at
the Sites that prompt Hallucinations of expanses of Time,
and from that Sacred Connection with the Past*

Artisan

I AM Fascinated by the Mystery & Magic of the Lost Civilisations –
Their Mighty Edifice upon which We base Our Existence to date.

I Was Rejoicing in History at the Pillars of Athens & Rome,
and Saw Architects' Eternity in Medieval Brick & Stone.

I Felt Untold beauty around the Statues of Renaissance,
and Dreamt in God's Flowering Windows of Gothic Cathedrals.

I've Counted Stars at night with Trees of the New town parks
and Known Naivety & Freedom in Colour-shaped modernity.

I See, We Are Natures Variety, Life's Imagination
through Art, where Feeling The World's charm,
Awakens the Joy of an
Open Heart

*   *   *

"When you travel, you become a better citizen of the planet.

It's not us versus them.

*It's about how we are going to handle this together,
get the most out of our lives, tolerate each other,
celebrate our differences, and put ourselves
in the mindset where we're more likely
to build bridges and less likely
to build walls."*

Rick Steves

The World

It is amazing how much Life You can put into one day!

Every step I make on this Sacred Earth is Appreciated,
Recognised, and Blessed. It is Done With Feeling!
It's Every Citizen is Honoured.

Every Street, Square, and Building is thus
known through the Light of Consciousness,
Iconised in pictures of my mind.

I have always been professional in my Voyage,
living the experiences of the Earth, enjoying places, reality,
meaning, writing, feeling, atmosphere, just Being!
Its importance in Space & Time. Her incredible
Heritage, Cultural and Natural Richness.

I was Walking through History, Past, Present, and Future,
and I did it in my unique, all-encompassing style.

Being constantly inspired to Live this larger-than-Life
adventure ensures You'll always be innovative
towards Living the Life of Your dreams!

After dissecting every city, village, and town,
every river, tree, rock, and blade of grass,
You cherish every thought, intent, and action
for being the product of a cause, and rightfully so.

The journey took me farther & faster than I could have ever imagined!

A journey filled with Adrenaline rushes, Transcendental & Enlightened
realisations, and larger-than-Life moments of Standing in awe,
of the Real-time Art of Creations.

Travelling is Fun, Educational, and Self Inspirational.

It Pushes You to keep seeing new horizons,
to stand on that shoreline, to be on that cliff walk,
to walk the forest path, to look from the mountain top,
to eat in that restaurant bar, to feel that cultural hype!

To explore those cities, villages, and towns, those squares,
churches, museums, and temples. To meet new People.

Sharing of such Worldly Magic as Knowledge in all forms
is the Most Important Service to Humanity One can Give!

*"Travel like Gandhi, with simple clothes, open eyes and
an uncluttered mind."* **Rick Steves**

With that Openness,
I have the Universe in my Eyes,
Eternity on my Mind,
Mercy in my Heart and Grace of my Soul.
For that, the World Loves me back Immensely.
Because I Know & Love The World,

Immeasurably

*   *   *

*I'll be at my office if You need me.
Or visit me at Home.*

*Of course,
You know the Way already.*

*There, behind the Magical
Doorway of the Universe*

CHAPTER6

LETTING GO

Back in Bliss

The Universe is a created part of nonexistence, the existing side of the non-dual Whole. The World is a holographic projection from the corner of the Universe, and You, as Consciousness, are a pixel part as well as the source of the projection. You are both manifested & unmanifested.
We dream of Ourselves sleeping into reality and
waking up from the mirage of individuality.

If You could experience reality from the more basic view, the particle level, there would be a mash of vibrational geometrical colours and the uniformity of the sense of Oneness. There would Be Consciousness. That is what mystics talk about when the ego is absent, what mediums bring forth from connection and channel to the Spirit world, what scientists observe at the fundamental level, and what the public is reporting & describing in the near-death and out of body experiences, psychedelic trips, plus all other spiritual illuminations & liberations.

These are undeniable pointers that We live in the Mental Universe, where We dream Ourselves into tangible reality, within subatomic possibilities, in Consciousness. These are *God's mysterious ways*, waking up to the *Maya*, the illusion of reality, *The Ten Thousand Things*. Such manifestations in the conscious possibilities of creation bring about God's realisation as the holy sacredness of the Source essence. Hence, He is every person, and all things culminated. God is the Oneness That IS.

The act of creation is remembering the past and future possibility that is already here. It is tapping into the Akashic records of Cosmic imagination, and by feeling it, We manifest it in the form of art and as Life itself. I'm not writing this book as much as Remembering it, as it already exists in the Vastness of the Now presence. I'm pulling out the sensible explanation of Quantum mechanics' *Many-worlds interpretation* from this Source Field. So You see, Our Conscious intuition corresponds with the current scientific investigations. By crossing the event horizon, We are closer to the Unification of the Whole, subject/object, big & small.

We are deleting the transparent boundary of the Sacred geometry, which no longer divides Us from Infinity. Here, We meet God in the form of You and in the shape of me. We don't stray from the moments' perseverance; We stay as the natural bright of Light, in the ecstasy that Our Souls bring, in the solitude of One's presence, abiding as Awareness.

This freedom is Divine, this joy innate/inherent; All are welcome to bathe in its nourishing kind-heartedness. What can You lose but limitations of falseness, the baggage of personal stories, or the heaviness of holding on to pain? Undress Yourself from fear in bondage, stay in Sunshine, touch the starlight of Your glowing heart, come Back to Bliss, and empower Thyself to be the person You can always count on as the Self of selves.

Wherever We stray from Bliss and find Ourselves in the destitution of seeming separation, We return to adhering to the punctual routine of holding on to thoughts, disrupting engagement in ceaseless desires of mind/body/ego characterisations, the addictions to sensory stimuli, ignoring the flower garden of inner beauty, of intrinsic peace, whose absence took Us going through the dark alleys of an unhappy childhood, to bullying in school, relationships with no connections, in fear of being alone, leading to disorderly family, jobs We don't like, friends We do not have, beliefs that are someone else's, a lifetime of chasing happiness, watching other people live, but not living Our dreams.

But if You could know such joy as being free, the freedom that I knew, the one I speak of, We would dance in the vibrational sequence of every subatomic particle, every quantum, every string of this supermembrane melody of God, and sing the odes to silence. We would hug & kiss the beloved in Us and caress Our Souls by indulging in thoughts of nonexistence. Ooh, how lonesome the symphony of the Universe is, for there is only One of Us ever truly Here. But how freeing this liberation feels, like Sunshine absent of clouds, as warm as a blanket on the bed of commingling angels, and the promise of sleepless paradise which lifts the migraine of separation and brings Us home,

back to the bliss of Source, back in bliss of the Self

InLightEnd

As You go into Meditation and drop Your character,
keeping the gentle smile, the mind/thoughts will follow.
With that, the Idea of the World falls apart, like the Matrix!
You then realise all is just a dream and all that We believe
is real is based on collective stereotypes.

When You look at a car, a tree, or a galaxy, what
You're seeing is an object in Consciousness, and that
their labels are merely words and terms describing the object.
The things themselves are Nameless. So once You strip Your mind
of this naming habit, looking without labelling will remain, which is
a liberating way to perceive things. It is Awareness' True nature.

Upon experiencing such liberating states in Consciousness,
Your Being Tunes into the Middle Way of Everything.
You become Awakened, naturally, through that
simple act of Observation, in Meditation!

This realisation of the True Self is the Greatest
Mystery that all the Great Teachers were pointing to.

*"Letting go gives us freedom, and freedom is the only condition
for happiness. If, in our heart, we still cling to anything; anger, anxiety,
or possessions, we cannot be free."* **Thich Nhat Hanh**

Once You get hold of It, once the ego goes, the
choice to remain as Peace will be Present.

Then, One considers not Himself,
but The World!

And can Remain
InLightEnd

Abandon all effort

Abandon all effort, mental & physical.

Don't even bother closing Your eyes!

Just focus on the object in front of You,
and Gaze at it without moving Your Eyes.

Doing this will make You realise how all the feelings
of unease associated with Life come from identifying with
the present experience, with the thinker, but in truth, You
are simply the Awareness of being aware of them.

*"How people treat you is their karma;
how you react is yours."* **Wayne Dyer**

You are then experiencing the pure state of
looking without judgment about thoughts, and in
such a process, You, as an idea of a separate self, Dissolve!

Your Fundamental Innate Nature then Shines Forth!
This is a Simple Fact of Being Aware and Present.

And People are unaware of how much They're holding on to mental &
physical patterns & behaviours and material & psychical possessions and
relationships. They hold on to an ideological image of Themselves and go
through life believing They are the sum of what They do, how They look,
what They are thinking, and of what Society has taught Them to feel.
They spend Their entire Life in routine, unaware of the Ocean of Life
Source hidden in front of every image, thought, and feeling. Such a way
of perceiving the World comes mainly from the monetary system. Most
People work hard to secure a livelihood, and that scarcity mindset is
forcing Them to place excessive value on temporary, external things.
Not many People are free from such a working/possessing system.

If everything were free and We lived in abundance, there would be no need for private property. But in this system, We hold on to things and see them as an extension of Ourselves. We are bound to suffer from the fate of these objects. People who have little are often happier than those who possess & hold on to things. Poor people with nothing to hold on to have nothing to lose. And We don't have to renounce possessions, but We can learn to be free of them. We can do that by detoxing and breaking addictions by slowly introducing a different lifestyle. Detoxing Our body & mind is a powerful & liberating way to Let Go of what's not serving Our wellbeing. We will see that Our core identity as an aware Being is always present, and that its happiness is not dependent on the outside World, on ideas, or possessions.

I recommend starting Your detox days free from any idea or needs. When You wake up, first become aware of Your breathing. Take long, deep breaths and be grateful for the self-control and Consciousness that You Are. Then, while brushing Your teeth, stay aware of it, feel the water, movements, and scents. After that, go to the place where You feel most comfortable and free to remain in the peace and quiet of Your Being. The same goes for partners and families. Arrange Your Life to feel connected and in peace wherever You want, need, and choose to.

Then instead of checking Your phone or TV, remain in the peace You have awakened into. Such morning stillness can be in the form of a prayer, but be sure to stay aware of every thought & action. Skip the breakfast and notice how the body reacts. More importantly, notice the arising mental reactions & commentaries.

You can write or read, but don't engage in any other productive action; leave everything as it is. Go for a walk in Nature. Feel how this peace underlies all of Life and how it is always here, every day, every moment. Relax into the freedom of doing nothing.

This moment, this entire day, You are the very presence of Life, with no attachments, no holding on to People or things. Don't even engage in conversation. Remain as the silent witness of the mind & The World.

You are aligned with the Timeless Being that You essentially Are.

Stay in this freedom for entire or several days, as often as You can.
Follow it with a juice and raw food diet or skip lunch & dinner too,
especially if You have extra weight; enjoy the freedom from eating
in the newfound lightness. Finish Your night in serene calmness.

It is important not to force this detox. There can't be resistance;
We must do it of Our own free will and enjoyment, to experience
the immediate benefits of lightness, peace, and bliss. Then,
We'll want to recreate such a state and feeling more often.
All the fasting, relaxing, retreating, letting go, and non-engaging
establishes Consciousness as the primary aspect of Your Being.

We don't waste energy on pleasing Our ego from such a free space,
instead, We focus on things that matter. We don't watch TV but invest
time into gardening, for example. We don't fight what is; We go
with the flow. We're not victims of the mind; We are aware Beings.
Aware of Our diets, bodies, and breath. We become conscious of
Our unconscious patterns, and We adapt according to the
intelligence of Consciousness. By mastering Yourself,
You will be the Master of the Universe.

As You learn to balance such days with family, work,
and Life in general, You will become a walking meditation.
You'll always be detoxing, wearing the smile & peace of God.
The closest comparison We can draw is a Flower or a Tree.
They're Alive, they Grow, but they have no interests other than
the Only One that is inscribed to them by their Very Nature.

As One lets go of attachments, concepts, and language
– Awakening, thus allowing natural silence to prevail
– Enlightenment, then trance-like mystification,
witnessing, and beingness remain.
That is freedom – Liberation!
The Isness of NOW

Let Go and Be

Simply & Completely Let Go!
Let It Go!

Suppose You Can Let Go of Everything!
All the ideas, concepts, relationships, beliefs,
all the feelings of lack and illusions of separation.

If You could allow Yourself the freedom from Yourself,
where the limited, static, personal sense of self is therein lifted,
leaving You with NOTHING, allowing You to realise how
this newfound observation of expanded Awareness
was all this time skilfully disguised within You,
in front of every thought, which Now gives You
all this Space, therefore giving You EVERYTHING!

Humanity's greatest teachers are the Same!
Buddha is a peaceful Jesus, and Jesus is a loving Buddha.
They are embodied representatives of One God,
expressing Their Universal Nature on Earth.

*"When we are still, looking deeply, and touching the source of
our true wisdom, we touch the living Buddha and the living Christ
in ourselves and in each person we meet."* **Thich Nhat Hanh**

You are The Christ Consciousness,
You have The Buddha Nature,
as Your Essence.
You Are The Light!

Don't just follow Jesus or Buddha;
be Jesus & Buddha in Your unique way.
Be the One You are waiting for to save You,
and there will be nothing left to save You from.

Was it not said that *God and Me are One,*
and that *You shall do these things and even greater?*

But don't flatter Your ego, as You're not a God. Rather,
God is Himself, through You! And all the more, as You
lower Your ego, God will Shine forth as Your Soul of Light.

You've been running around Your entire Life, chasing success and
happiness, Dear Human, while ignoring the One Truth that You can only
find by sitting with Yourself, by allowing Your mind to cease the noise, thus,
revealing the One Fundamental Isness of Your Self-aware Being.

"All of humanity's problems stem from man's inability to
sit quietly in a room alone." **Blaise Pascal**

All of Our problems arise as doubting thoughts since We're
lowering Ourselves by questioning Our worth. You don't see
flowers thinking less of themselves than what they are, and they
are still & beautiful. So know Yourself as the Peace & Beauty which
Humans are, as Soul Essence and Light as Conscious Participants.

"If you love a flower, don't pick it up. Because if you pick it up, it dies,
and it ceases to be what you love. So if you love a flower, let it be.
Love is not about possession. Love is about appreciation." **Osho**

In recognition of Your Essential Nature as Pure Awareness, as
the flowering beauty, there is neither a You which needs to be right,
nor is there a You which needs anything other than this Being.

You are that basic and simple Awareness of Being.
You are the Knowing of Your Own Self.
You Are The Beingness Itself.

Just Be That!
Be It.
Be

126

Transcendence

By inviting and allowing more presence in Our Lives, We develop the ability to drop the identity and abide as the Awareness, which is available limitless, We are setting the stage for the higher and more meaningful purpose of Our Lives: Consciousness.

"The meaning of life is just to be alive. It is so plain and so obvious and so simple. And yet, everybody rushes around in a great panic as if it were necessary to achieve something beyond themselves." **Alan Watts**

Transcendence of the egoic mind-made boundaries is the ultimate lasting experience within Our culturally narrowed states of existence. It is the beginning of freedom from Ourselves & The World where We can always stay contemplative and aware of that broader medium in which everything happens, in which Our Souls naturally reside.

What We are Transcending is all of the sense of identity that can't withstand the Conscious scrutiny, the Presence of Awareness, the Love of the Heart or the Knowledge of a Liberated mind.

We are also Letting Go of the sense of regional belonging, of Our proud cultural heritage, nevertheless always honouring it for giving Us the necessary moral and artistic footprints, but Transcending it for the greater good of Humanity, as mirroring Universal freedom in order to be empty above the Cosmic Space of Infinite Awareness, provides limitless possibilities for existing and creating.

We're leaving behind all the feelings of accomplishment, all the prejudices outside the known cultural conditioning. In this way, We'll meet and approach all further and new interactions with ultimate appreciation for Living Beings. One will be felt in every Other Living Being, with no fear of rejection, no thoughts, no time, only knowledge of the common deeper Being.

Coming together from such an open and free attitude towards Life,
Our Peace is Present, Our Love Awakens, Our Breath is Alive!

As Consciousness takes the driving seat and speeds up the intelligence
evolution, by virtue of fearlessness and ascending the patriarchal and
materialistic efforts of ego, Our True Selves are shining ever so outwardly.

As We effectively invite the presence of Awareness through meditation,
contemplation, and prayer, those natural wheels of Life, the Chakras,
reopen, subsequently allowing divine purpose to enfold within Our
expanded Awareness, which is the ever-present Consciousness.

*"Life exists only at this very moment, and in this moment it is infinite
and eternal, for the present moment is infinitely small; before we can
measure it, it has gone, and yet it exists forever... ."* **Alan Watts**

This effort at stillness, and of no resistance, brings out Our
required Life energy. Such intensity of the presence Transmutes
closed-mindedness into Openheartedness, jealousy into Loving
unconditionally, and proudness of the ego into the Prowess of Oneness.

This vast freedom from Yourself allows You to discover the richness in
the healing and nurturing Light so that You can let go of all shadowy
scraps and settle all the disputes. This is the Light of being still, and
within that, Free. Free to accept the choiceless journey of losing One's
lostness, of finding One's egolessness, of Transcending Oneself
from careless imperfection into graceful readiness

*   *   *

*All of this magic vibrates within Us, as the Universe wants to
express itself through Our Conscious channel; Our loving hearts.
It wants to feel One as it naturally is, and We can help this
miracle by lowering Our egos, by facing Our fears
by facing Ourselves in Others, with Love*

Rainbow

It is said that a picture is worth a thousand
words. So let's put that statement to the test!

Once, I witnessed a whole incredible Rainbow
but didn't have my phone to take a photo of it. So
I will describe it to You, in roughly 1,000 words:

I'm standing in front of a mid-size aeroplane.
This plane is a Human miracle of technology.

What You see right now is an incredible
spectacle of Light & Weather, a fantastic array
of colours shaped in a half-circular tubular dome,
creating the phenomenon We know as a Rainbow.

This Wonder presents a Natural Miracle of Nature!

So there it is. Precisely above the plane, half circling it
from the ground to the ground like a Saint's halo, with
a backdrop of spectacular weather patterns with clouds
shaping, morphing, and forming, materialising a soft, thin
mirage in gentle rain veil of droplets, reflecting the magical
prism of Light and projecting it as an astonishing Rainbow.

There is a line of passengers boarding the plane. Some are
walking with Their heads down, trying to miss this soft rain,
exaggerating the mild weather conditions, glorifying Their
egos, playing the victim by feeling sorry for Themselves,
and blaming Nature for disrupting Their easy walkway
into the plane. They are completely ignorant of the
actual Miracle playing just above Their heads.

They are entirely missing the Present moment,
by acting out the identification with Their minds.
These are players.

While some Others are experiencing the full
Sight which is unfolding in front of Them.

They're stopping Their friends, partners, kids,
pointing fingers at the Event, marvelling,
feeling instantly astonished,
Awakened, and Overwhelmed.

And They're not missing out on the Fun, oh no!
They are taking photos, recording video clips, and making the
most of that Moment by capturing the Essence of Presence.

Iconising it for later, showing Others and preserving a
Natural Miracle, the point in Space & Time, where They
witnessed such Goodness of Living so Open Heartedly.

Their Faces are Smiling, Joyful!
Their Hearts Overflowing with Magical Ecstasy,
a Worldful Presentation for the Soul Senses.
But above all, those Untouched by the same World.
Those spanning Time & Space, Sacred & Holy,
Real & Illusory, Solid & Empty, Existing & Devoid.
From the Source; in the Source; by the Source;
Always & Forever; Never & Now.

And how can this Deepness of Universal Scale of
things not be detected by You, a Point in Infinity?
Facing just what is in front of You,
to show You Again and Forever
if You are Present enough to See it,
how You Too are the Silent Witness,
even if You're a victim of conditions.

And so You, my Dear, my Love!
You are standing in front of Everything,
Gazing into a Magnificent Tapestry,
into minutia details of Sights & Scenes.
And even though You don't have a phone to capture it,
it is there, Forever Etched into Your Heart's Eyes,
like a Glowing River in the Sky,
Freely Flowing by not adding anything to it,
but easily Letting Go of any influences,
by simply Being, to See.

You, my Dearest, are the Essence of this Event!
Which is tHere, in its Natural form, Untouched, Unspoiled
by outside preconceived notions of stereotypical behaviour of
minds, bodies, egos, and You are the Reflecting Mirror of
that sweet digestible addiction to spice up the moment
with Your Soul's Language, in Love with Life.

Yes, this is the Essential Teaching!
To open Your Heart's pockets and let them
overflow with Grace & Mercy, as Kindness,
Tenderness, Gentleness, Sensitivity,
Compassion, Giving, and Caring.

For it is tHere that, in the Authenticity of Your
Own Shining Brilliance, We find the True Freedom,
an Ever-existing Intoxicating Fluid of Source Energy,
quietly Kissing the bare Feet of Others' Souls!

You & I are so Fond of this New Found Freedom, which
doesn't neglect anyone or anything in Existence anymore
but Embraces Them with the Full Force of Awareness.

This Intensity of staying Present is the Intent of Flying
Conscious into the Ever-expanding Hallways of the Heart,
throughout the Mind Storms of Spirits' Quest for God.

Because it's not about not caring anymore, it's about
Caring for All the Right things, my Dears!

Awaken Your Full potential by expressing how it Feels to be You!

Your unique experience is all that ever matters, Dear One,
and together with Everyone else's, it's creating a
New World Community of Young Lovers in Art.

It is when You Gaze like this, into the Wilderness of
Universal Variety – a Superposition of Possibilities in Action,
that reveal what is possible when Atoms Start Kissing
and Sculpturing the Fabric of Multiversal Realities or
Non-realities – that We Awaken Our True Purpose.

You will then Fly in an Ecstasy of Refusing to
Give up on these Abnormalities, which are
softly Caressing Your Soft-spots of Laughter.

& Oh, I don't think We can reach 1,000 words in a picture.
And You know what? I do not intend to! I want to leave
some Space for later because We've already peaked at
the Infinitesimal number of Planck scales, Non-binary,
& Non-dual; what is the Biggest possible number Here?

All of this Wisdom is the Poetry of Forever's Knowing
of the type of pleasure for the Formless Senses that You
can Enlighten with the Light of Your Presence.

You can Lighten-up with the image Outward,
or You can Light-Yourself-up, zooming Inward.

All of this, my Love, is a Scenario in that one Photo
that You will Never See but that You can forever Taste if You
step outside of trying to understand the Why & How and
Undress Yourself in the Art of *LETTING GO!*

This one Photo is Staring at You with Your every breath. This Super
Image, that will never be captured by Human technology
is being Divinely Ceremonialised Here, in Yourself,
as a Reflection of what's Right in Front of You.

An Eternal Ever-present Quality of
Experiencing What Is. A Formless Essence!
But above All, a Picturesque Landscape
of Artisans various shapes & forms.
In Love with The World.
In a graceful touch that can Now
be Known as You and Me.

I want to whisper this Aliveness to You, Dear Reader,
while painstakingly brushing away all that was hurt, all
that was neglected when You got a little drunk with
separating Yourself with beliefs in Here & There,
Us & Them, Mine & Yours, Can'ts & Don'ts!

So Kiss these Cheeks of Playfulness of Your
Innermost Beloved Child again, while the
Entire World Dances in front of Us in
the form of this Fascinating Rainbow.

And in front of the Rainbow,
The World is making Love
in the Image & Likeness

of the Beautiful You

*   *   *

Abide in the Bliss You have Inside,
Be the Peace You are Within

It Doesn't Matter

It doesn't matter what's happening at
the Edge of the Universe or in another Galaxy.
Nor does it matter what the other Star Civilisations are
up to. It neither matters what China and India are doing nor
the Americans. There is Nothing You can do about Africa either.
You shouldn't care about what Your neighbouring countries
are doing, or, for that fact, even Your neighbours.
It is all just a passing thought. Chances are:

We're All Going to Go having had no influence on it!

In the recognition that no thoughts about the past
matter and no dreaming about the future counts,
You focus on the quality of the Present task,
staying in the good feeling of being Yourself,
and lose any need to overthink, dwell, or feel pity,
by virtue of accomplishing Your moment's Life.

The only thing that matters In the End is Your Own
Space, Peace, and Love. Your Own Knowledge.
And in such Absence of the World,
Your Authentic Self

*   *   *

"The individual has always had to struggle to
keep from being overwhelmed by the tribe.
If you try it, you will be lonely often,
and sometimes frightened.
But no price is too high to pay for
the privilege of owning yourself."
Friedrich Nietzsche

The True Self

How can You Take Your Life from thinking to Knowing?

Before thought, before the mind, there is a natural state of
Presence, of Being, of Life. That state is the Knowing
Being! It requires no thought to know it.
No thoughts can know this!
Only Being Knows Itself.

Being already Is; You need to Stop resisting it!
How You do it: Feel It; Be It; Know It; Be Being.
Focus on the Inner Feel, the Aliveness in the Body,
the Breath, and the Conscious Attention of Awareness.

It is in this most Intimate and Peaceful state of Being that the
Knowing of Wellness is gladly perceived, with no judgment of
Self or Others, only the Graceful Understanding of Everyone's
Needs and Right for the experience.

There is nothing new to learn, but concentrate on What Is
already Here, what Was, and Always Will Be.

Unlearn all the mind and belief stuff; Be what You naturally Are.

Free Yourself from ego, from all the ideas of Right & Wrong,
Good & Bad, Beautiful & Ugly – Just Be!

That is Your innate Wisdom, and the Purpose
of Life is to Know Yourself as That. To Be Thyself.

That is a fundamental nature of perception and it's not reserved
for the select few as You can Access and Know it in Every Moment
of Your Life. Draw Your attention away from the next thing You want
to do on to the very thing that You are doing Now. Be in The Now.

*Once We realise the True Self as Peace, Unconditional
Love is the state which remains, and it shines forth naturally.*

Everything else is a thought-inflicted egoism of personality. The origin
of the word 'Persona' even means to sound through a mask, as the Ancient
Greeks used masks in theatres to personify the various states of mind.

That is The Freedom from Space & Time, from Your personal
Story or History! Freedom to be Free from unconsciousness.
And Consciousness is the Awareness.

That is the Jesus' Kingdom of Heaven: Sky, implying Openness,
Vastness, Space. It doesn't come, nor can it be found There.
It is Always Here & Now, the Only True Existence.

Or Buddhist Nothingness, or Emptiness, which is Consciousness.
It is All & Nothing!

Everything else is a passage of thoughts, the illusion of a
Self-created mind. Noticing this brings Peace and is not
something You need to practice, learn, create, awaken, or
contemplate. It is Who You are in Essence and is already
within You as the Consciousness in which the World appears.

"When we let go of all expectation, there is peace." **Kim Eng**

Awareness of breathing is the entry point to Peace,
and it is unchangeable, unmanifested, eternal, and constant.
Everything arises in and recedes into Peace, into Silence.

*The only way to Die and Rest in Peace is to Live in Peace.
If You want to go to Heaven, You must Live as if You are in Heaven already!*
And We Are, if We Align Ourselves with this state of Pure Perception.

That is The Secret, The Holy Grail, Nirvana, or Bliss that
all Traditions, Religions, and Wisdom teach Us!

Know Thyself as Wakeful Beingness, and Everything else Will Be Known!

By Considering Yourself and Waking up from the dream of thoughts,
or the mind-made self, the ego, You've found the True Self and, by that,
You've changed Yourself, and in that, You have Considered the World.

*"Finding that core of truth within yourself... That truth that knows and
trusts that All Is Well, and that chooses Love... Is the greatest
spiritual attainment you can ever make."* **David Wilcock**

The mind has created the World which seeks Love & Truth
outside of Itself, and We end up twisting Love & Truth.
We've turned it from Being to doing, from Knowing to seeking.

The fear of the unknown forces Us to fit in with the masses.
We have identified with the thought, the form, and the idea.
We've given all of Our Attention to the World in ignorance.

*"Do not fear the unknown. The unknown is where the rest
of you resides. The only thing you will discover there
is more of yourself."* **Bashar/Darryl Anka**

Managing Our fears is The Spiritual Journey.
We Thrive by not being afraid of Who We Are.

In the face of fear, Smile, keep a confident stare
and eye contact; feel what You Are and say it proudly.
All You Need and Are is Your Consciousness of Love.

*When People get together with this intent in Their Hearts,
of seeing Divinity in Everything, and sharing Love
with All God's Creations, Miracles Happen!*

Now, take back the Attention
to Your Inner
Being

CHAPTER 7

AWAKENING

The Knowing Being

"Breathing in, I calm my body. Breathing out, I smile.
Breathing in, there is only the present moment.
Breathing out, it is a wonderful moment."
Thich Nhat Hanh

Breathe! Focus the Attention on that,
5 seconds In, and 5 seconds Out.

Sense within Yourself
how it feels to be in Your body,
in Your Consciousness.

Now, let the body Breathe for itself.
Don't control it, but follow it with Awareness.

How Does It Feel to Be the body,
As Consciousness?

That is Who You Are!
The Knowing Of Being,
THE KNOWING BEING

*   *   *

The World is literally Your Mirror!
Whatever You put out is reflected back.

If You are criticising, You are the criticism.
If You are hating & blaming, You are the pain.

If You are smiling into the mirror, it smiles back!
If You're kind, patient, and loving, You are the Bliss

Philosophy

Philosophy is the thinking science about the World that is separate from the standpoint of the freed mind. How do We tackle such a vast subject in a few pages without having to ignore half of it to focus on the best of the latest thinkers in the area of Our conscious interests: Existentialism!

Life, in its essence, is & should be as simple as living quietly and doing no more than needed while having no thoughts. When a need arises, We observe it and if it doesn't pass, We satisfy it, by drinking, eating, sleeping, etc., before morality kicks in and defies Us for these natural inclinations, complicating the World to the point of good & evil. So to know better, We should provide the means to cater for all those needs, hence We work on securing them. Growing & gathering food is, therefore, the basis for any Life preservation since it is Our primary need. Once You separate from the food You eat, You are separate from Life essence. You are then, by definition, lost in the World, to ponder and engage in matters that are not essential for Being. You overlook the very being of essence that You became separate from.
The person who is the Being is essentially not interested in essence, for a such person is already one with Being, and Being precedes essence. Its means justify the end, or *it's not about the destination but the journey*. Thinking about thinking will not solve thinking problems.

Being Is, by being It, is achieved by relaxing the essential needs. We are the Being. Being doesn't organise itself; it doesn't stray from Nature; it melts back into the Beingness. By separating Ourselves from Nature, We are driven by doing, not Being. Civilisation is, therefore, a product of unconscious lostness in unnatural needs, which is the product of doing and the loss of Being.
All the history exists because We can't recognise and surrender Our needs and voices back to Being. But Life has a solution for that in its grand design: physical death. Thus, making sure We are reminded that the Being underly doing. For this reason, Philosophy is bound to surrender to Spirituality. And thinking into knowing & being the Being.

We seem to perceive Existence only because We have fallen asleep into doing and separated the Being by thinking. Time is the by-product of this individual sense of the thinker. Time is the result of losing the Being and thoughts are the cause of it. The World & Existence are comprised of focused light and exist in Our imagination. The senses and brain catalyse the light and create the World by reconstructing its image in the imagination. We can alter the resulting imagination by changing Our beliefs or by nonidentifying with the image, but this rarely ever happens. We are yet to see the 'moving of mountains.'

However, We know it can be done because the World is illusory. We simply lack the primary freedom from self-perception since it is limited by basically everything. We perceive and persist on the identity of perception. And even without perception, We still hold on to the sense of the perceiver. Physical death again is the illusion destroyer. We just need to suffer or indulge for a lifetime before We can be liberated by it.

Follow Your deep breathing and relax the mind into Being.

Philosophy often has a pessimistic and nihilistic view of existence, describing it as the circle of pleasure and suffering. The mind is prone to seek completion & fulfilment through pleasure, but when that is unsatisfied or even desired, suffering is the effect.

> *"Every existing thing is born without reason, prolongs itself out of weakness, and dies by chance."* **Jean-Paul Sartre**

If Life is not already hard enough, They add this impossible existential burden to it. It feels like a continuing dread of utter purposelessness, an inescapable trap of unwillingness to live, of meaninglessness in engaging in any mode of societal behaviour, lacking in appetite, joy, smiles, and thoughts, steeped with the misery of One's existential prospect of death. The system is heavy, People are unapproachable, relationships impossible, living unbearable, depression constant, the pain energy-robbing, therefore, the end is welcomed as if it's Life itself, all of which is the result of *Existential angst.*

> *"Human existence is an error...it is bad today and every day it gets worse, until the worst happens."* **Arthur Schopenhauer**

We seem to perceive an indivisible multiplicity of objects & things, but there is really only *emptiness dancing*. The consequence of staying too long in seeing the illusion is that the mind loses its grip on reality and can subsequently become unable to function within society.

"If you're lonely when you're alone, you're in bad company." **Jean-Paul Sartre**

Nietzsche's insight expresses this:
"peak and abyss they are now joined together," and,
"if you gaze long enough into an abyss, the abyss will gaze back into you."

Some paint a different picture and embrace Life by keeping lively spirits. They are one action ahead of boredom, cheerfully ahead of dwelling in pain, using communication ahead of loneliness.

"Be kind, for everyone you meet is fighting a hard battle." **Socrates**

It is a dance and a balance that We learn through experience, and it is something We need to be educated about. *"Life is not a problem to be solved, but a reality to be experienced."* **Soren Kierkegaard**

The community of like-minded Souls is a paradise for such seekers, but in the absence of it Life can seem like living in hell.
"My principle article of faith is that one can only flourish among people who share the identical ideas and the identical will." **Nietzsche**

Not One individual should be excluded from achieving Their highest purpose. For this reason, We must educate Ourselves and Others to the True nature of the *I*, of the Self, of Awareness that is Consciousness.

In the moment of utmost serenity, and complete peace, the individual *I* is recognised as a thought, idea, sense, or feeling. So it is not real, that is to say, it is temporary or illusory. In the points of recognition and in total calmness, it is not tHere. What is Here is the knowing and Remembering of Nothing. *I* that knows, is the *I* that disappears in the Centre as Consciousness, until there is no *I* left to claim the knowledge of anything.

Ramana Maharshi calls this, *I-I*. And **Socrates**, *I know that I know nothing*.

Nietzsche reflected on this freedom from *I*: *"How calmly all things lie in the light! How freely one breathes! How much one feels lies beneath oneself!"* He also said, *"What finally comes home to me is my own self,"* and further remarks, *"all things are baptized in the well of eternity,"* by seeing the infinite nothingness.

By investigating the concept of *I*, many intellectuals have struck philosophical gold. Their existentialist efforts paid off by giving Them glimpses of freedom from Themselves. As with most spiritual seekers, the freedom is short lasting but it is powerful and profound enough to alter and change the course of Their lives. They can never be the same *I* after They have peaked beyond the Self.

Today, We have such experiences daily, in meditation or in spontaneous moments of clarity & calmness while remaining still, by devoting to the empty mind and the pure heart of liberated teachers, and by melting Our ego in the radiant love of a relationship, parenthood, or community. But the one True authentic space of recognition is Your own complete peace. You don't go anywhere; Your mind is not in an altered state.

Consciousness simply is as It Is. The one
undeniable reality is the presence that It IS.

In looking at the mind, We are the looking.
In observing the World, We are observance.
In comprehending reality, We are the totality.

We are the permeating presentness, nonengaging
satisfactoriness, completion of the fullness, and
the voice of the quietness which speaks in silence

*   *   *

"Being and time determine each other reciprocally, but in such a manner that neither can the former - Being −be addressed as something temporal nor can the latter - time −be addressed as a being." **Martin Heidegger**

Meaning of Life

Lots of people derive Their meaning in Life from Their Religion, from
a belief that God started the Universe for the Soul's reason of allowing
Humanity to develop and have a Spiritual relationship with Them,
similar to how We have a relationship with Our children & families.
So, in a way, We are part of the ultimate divine family. Other people
are purely materialistic or strive only for comfort and pleasure.

But however deeply One might ponder this, or any meaning to Life,
One can not help but notice how such relationships or ideas are based
solely on a belief. Either a belief in the spiritual or material Worlds.

From a Conscious point of view, the Material World is an appearance
within its knowledge of itself. There is no separation, and there is no
duality; there is only One Consciousness experiencing Itself individually
through the Universe, and through whatever other realities & existences
there might be.
In this way, it's only through experiencing & understanding this Oneness
for Yourself, and through recognising the True nature of Consciousness,
that One eliminates the need to believe or see reality as separate.

To find the True Meaning in Life, We must seek that ultimate knowledge
of Ourselves and Our Place in the World. As Nature is Our Mother,
forget about the Father. Nature must be Our first meaning in Life.
If We want to survive on this Earth, then Nature Must Survive. Nature
is more important than Humanity, for We can't survive without Her.

If We, however, manage to develop technology that will allow Us to
leave the Earth and use any other Planet's resources for survival, or
if We can live in spaceships and create matter & food from thin air,
then obviously Our meanings & values will change & adapt accordingly.
We can only respect God's creation or acknowledge the programmer's
simulation of the Universe, but as We are fully Conscious Beings
Ourselves, We have the responsibility to derive Our own meanings.

We must determine Our own meaning in Life, for every new generation.

So going back to the God question, God can never be the true source of meaning, for He is a fictional projection of Our history. And even if God does exist as a Universal Being, it still changes nothing. Identical to the way that children have Their own Lives independent of Their parents', They find meaning based on collective or personal understanding.

Of course, the Conscious meaning is always only dedicated to Life, to being Conscious. Conscious Life would never harm another Living Being for its benefits. So Conscious evolution almost certainly implies vegetarianism, in other words, the end of killing for meat consumption.

As a Conscious Being, knowing this for Yourself and having that feeling of Value for all Life gives You the infinite understanding of the only possible God's True nature, as Pure Consciousness. With that, We know that no moral and unconditionally loving God exists. If God existed as a Being, He would most certainly have a personality. The bigger the Being, the bigger the ego. *"God is Unconscious"* and the Bible is not shy there.

> *"The God of the Old Testament is arguably the most unpleasant character in all fiction: jealous and proud of it; a petty, unjust, unforgiving control-freak; a vindictive, bloodthirsty ethnic cleanser; a misogynistic, homophobic, racist, infanticidal, genocidal, filicidal, pestilential, megalomaniacal, sadomasochistic, capriciously malevolent bully."* **Richard Dawkins**

Whichever way We want to flip the God argument, We're talking about a powerful Alien being who created something or everything, including Us, but this gives Him no more divinity or gives Us no more reason to worship Him than good or bad parents deserve Our respect, fear, or love. Everything does deserve absolute and Conscious scrutiny though.

To base Your meaning on the possible existence of God is like saying that the only meaning to Your Life is the existence of Your parents.

The meaning of Life is Life Itself.

147

*"The greatest gift creation has given to all of you is that life is
fundamentally meaningless. That means it has no built-in meaning.*

*What that also means is, you were designed to give it the meaning
you prefer to give it. And the meaning you give it will utterly
determine how you experience it."* **Bashar/Darryl Anka**

We can live many types of lifestyles in many kinds of Universes,
but the only thing We can ever know is the Knowing of any such
Life experience. That knowing is the same in any Conscious Beings,
the same in Humans, in Aliens, and in God.

To talk about God from such a Conscious perspective or Truth is to
be romantic. So We must experience that feeling of Oneness, of Pure
Consciousness, that We call God. Still, this God is no more personal
than the illusory sense of Our individuality, as a belief in passing
thoughts, which is the only place where individuality can be found.

If We want to be precise and serious about making any God claims,
it's best to forget the entire idea altogether. If God is All or Nothing,
He is synonymous with Consciousness since only Consciousness is
aware. And whether it is aware of All or Nothing, it doesn't make the
Conscious importance. But it does matter if You want to ascribe the
fictional validity to it and claim God's presence or existence in it.

*"Enjoy the questions because they open many doors.
Forget the answers because they change all the time.
We are never going to understand the miracle of life.
Isn't that wonderful?"* **Paulo Coelho**

Nobody has ever, and nobody will ever, find any evidence
for the existence of matter, nor the presence of God.

We only know the very act of looking for it.
We only know the Conscious experience

New Paradigm

We measure spiritual success in the amount of peace One can abide in and it is all about living it authentically. There are no shortcuts or tricks here. We have to surrender, do the necessary practice, the healing, & feel the highest excitement with Our entire being. Do only what liberate You, feel it, and Be It deeply. We don't live Spirituality; We are Spirituality, a lifetime investigation of discovering One's True nature. And how could anybody want anything else than to be itself fully, as the awakening of the Soul? Now, it may be relatively easy to live such essence privately, but it is when We can interact with Others in the community on this liberating level that We feel the power of being alive and authentic Consciousness. That is when One starts becoming an honest Spiritual teacher. Here the students are more important than the teacher, for a teacher is already a realised Soul, and it is in Their grace to influence Others' realisation. In this delicate relationship, the teacher and student create the teaching. This is not about some imaginary goodness, rather, getting rid of ego and seeing what remains. A true teacher doesn't see themself as a teacher but as a corresponding conscious link in this reality of evolving Awareness.

We can track this progress of the Collective from the prehuman era when self-awareness in the ancient human was close to feral. As they began organising in larger communities, doing agriculture, with religion, and creating civilisations, awareness has awakened correspondingly since they had more time free from work. Humans began investigating different realms of existence in the role of shamans, chieftains, prophets, gurus, sages, philosophers, priests, monks, poets, artists, scientists, etc.

Today almost everybody has access to transcendental knowledge through education, religions, libraries, the internet, organisations, and movements. Collective Awareness of the Civilisations is rising ever so increasingly. Nations are mixing and the population is becoming One Global Family. Globalisation is the correct term, and a spiritual teacher is the fastest way for Civilisation to progress Consciously, for They strike at the source of problems and establish the basis for a New paradigm

Spirituality

All Life outside Love is Foolosophy!

*Foolosophy is philosophising to justify One's inability to Love,
as failing to connect with the True Self, to feel with the wide
World & Nature, not to separate Oneself from All. It's the
ego's addiction to the endless involvement in the World.*

There are countless Human-made philosophies,
religions, and ideas, while there is an infinite number
of Alien-created ways of Life too. But there is only
One Universal Truth underlying all those philosophies,
which is Consciousness, expressed in the Universe as
Nature, and in Humans as an Awareness, as Love, as God.

Spirituality is the most worthy of Human creations. It is the
Reunion with Our Soul, it is the Art of Conscious Living!

Spirituality is thus working on Our True nature.
It is the Sacred Life behind every form & shape;
it's the glue that makes inanimate matter Alive.
Word Spirit means to Animate, to Breathe.
Spirituality is the Life of Our Soul!

It is the inner engineering, the awakening of supreme intellect,
divine knowledge, graceful mercy, and compassionate action.

There are many levels to such an Awakening!
And We need to Awaken to all of these realities in Life.
The fundamental one is the Being, which is not separate from
Consciousness and being One with It is Enlightenment!

"Awakening cannot satisfy you. It frees you from the need to be satisfied."
Matt Kahn

Other Awakenings are on the intellectual or the mind level,
as well as that of the physical, feeling the true body functions
surrounding diet and exercise.
Then the economic and every other system of Human Civilisation.
And finally, Nature, the Raw Reality of the Natural World,
and distinguishing it from the Man-made System.

Spirituality is walking a Life of many Awakenings until We arrive
at the Perfect Centre, free of Our egos, at the Singularity of Our Souls.
Complete Awakening is to See & Know all of this momentarily.
All observed and freely enjoyed in Consciousness.

*"Awakening is the first stage of the process, second is
illumination, and the final stage is liberation."* **Shunyamurti**

If You're sharing this Community, this Country, this Continent,
this World with 8 billion People, and Existence, with an infinite
number of species in the Universe, then We are, by Nature,
all the Same, all One Big Worldly and Universal Family.

We'd be wise to find the Base of Spirituality Right Here & Now,
aligned with this fact of Existential Sharing because everything
else is just extrapolation on this Core Truth of Life.

That is Spirituality, to be Appreciative of Our Shared Being!

If this common appreciation for All of Life doesn't imply
Spirituality to You and doesn't Awaken Your Sense of Social &
Cosmological importance of compassionate acceptance, then We
need to Stop Here and Start again from the basics. We can not
treat a problem; We must cure the cause immediately at its root.

*To truly comprehend and excel at achieving this Sense of General
companionship with All forms of Life is the Key to Aligning Ourselves
with Our Soul Frequencies. It is what separates Us Humans from plants
and animals. It is nothing else, nothing more, and nothing less!*

You Awaken Your Soul throughout Your Lifetime by abiding
in the Base ground of perception, The Conscious Breath.

But We expend a great deal minding Ourselves too much,
instead of being Still and Free as All the Universe and Nature Are!

Once You stop pretending to be a Human who is separate from All
and instead relax in this nonstop Life-meter of the body; Breath,
You'll allow the Divine Essence inside You to experience
it within the World of Your perception freely.

We Live to sense & express this unique viewpoint of
Our apparent reality. With that, We are moving full circle in
recognition of Our True nature, and this Art of presenting those
truths then immortalises Us as an individual aspect of God.

That gives You the Freedom to manifest, to artistically express
as a Human Soul, as a Masterpiece of Honesty that We all have
and carry within Our most Sincere and Authentic True Selves.

This is the fundamental existential nature of Self-awareness.
That is the Miracle of being You, being One with Being,
in Love with Light!

"Walk through life in a sweet Awakening." **Matteo Passigato**

We should All embody this Life's inspirations and enjoy the
sweet taste of melting into it, thus losing the sense of separation.

*For You are another Me, and Everyone else's experience is the
main blockbuster movie on the Universe's holographic screen.*

How freeing and mending this appreciation is!

Spirituality is the Ultimate Philosophy of any Social & Sentient Beings.
It is the 'Ess' in the Mystery of Consciousness

Eternal Radiance

Everything is exactly as it should be and is right as it is. The Equilibrium of Status Quo is always balancing itself according to the energetic pulses of Consciousness at large. There is always a corresponding amount of equality between these forces; even if they could be placed and weighed on either side on a smaller scale, they'd eventually find the even level. Such a visual can be directly applied to the Universal extent of things, and on the individual Beings. They'll fluctuate between unconsciousness and peace, during this or theoretically many lifetimes until finding a middle ground as Consciousness.

Regardless of the possible agenda to keep the Human population living in ignorance & ego, the powers that be, with their rampage of control, are playing their part too. In a way, they are making this inevitable Awakening possible. They are the counterweight, the dark side of the ying-yang destiny of the Universe. All manifestations are ultimately a part of God returning to God. Given this understanding, there can't be any anger towards any party in Existence. Consciousness is only too aware of the bigger Universal picture, the manifested order of things, and the Cosmic ramifications of Self-aware Beings.

As such free Beings, it almost becomes Our spiritual duty to bring about this Conscious end for a new beginning. That is why You need to enjoy Your spiritual authenticity, as nobody has Your perspective in the World. It is Your purpose to embody it.

All religions & traditions talk about bringing this Kingdom of Heaven to Earth. That intent is described by Nietzsche as *The Will To Power* that lends itself to becoming the decent Human Beings that We are destined to be. Let's start inviting such Soul principles in practical language with an example of universally applied guidance for Spiritual attainment:

When You wake up in the morning, give Thanks to God, to the Universe, and to Life for giving You an opportunity to experience Existence as

loving Awareness. Take deep conscious breaths and feel this graceful
attitude of love in Your blissful heart. Do this for as long as is comfortable
or necessary to feel ready to abide in that appreciation throughout the day.

Let this day start with such meditation every morning.
Let this day end with such meditation every evening before sleeping,
and keep this blessing all day.

If You are coming from a religious or spiritual tradition,
You may already be doing this in the form and act of prayer.
If so, You can deepen the gratitude by intensifying the experience by
staying aware as You speak the prayer or mantra. Be the witness of this
and feel it already realised in Your heart. This is a gesture of constant
Falling into Grace and remaining an undeniable master of Your
immediate space, in conscious recognition.

In recognising Oneself as Consciousness, this very knowing frees You
from seeking external recognition and validation. You stay free from
outside influences, centred in the authority of One's unshakable being.
This authenticity of being present knows no time. It acts from its current
knowledge of inner peace, and it has no need to search for memories, so
it does not rush things; it performs in a relaxed, concentrated manner.

To enter such care-free abidance, keep returning to the awareness of
breathing. That is inseparable from Your true essence, and One can not
go behind this stare of radiance. That White Light is the Eternal Source
from which all Life comes into Being. That luminosity is One God in
all Universal expositions as Spirit.

If, however, the mere attendance of being present is not enough for You
to find peace, here is a practical example to bring You closer to God,
to Consciousness:
    Start writing down Your feelings of gratitude, Your gratefulness for
    being on this spiritual path of inquiry into the True nature of Yourself:

I acknowledge my sacred presence as waking Consciousness of this World.

*I honour You, God, for staying close to me as the Self That I AM.
From this mercy of non-resistance, this gift of self-control, I dedicate all
my waking, dreaming, and sleeping awareness to Your higher purpose,
which is manifesting Now through me. I Am eternally grateful for the
Beings in my vicinity; call Them partners, children, family, relatives,
friends, co-workers, and People of the World. I recognise the importance
of the Natural World; Soil, Water, Vegetation, Animals; The SUN
as the Life shining Light; & The White Radiance of Eternity.*

Write down such thankfulness of a healthy Soul in all forms of literacy.
Read them aloud, and recite these verses whenever it feels empowering
in the moment's joy. Learn them to the point of mantra or prayer.
This spiritual vocalisation will reverberate through Your
body's energy field, with the Power of Illumination.

Whether You awaken the light directly through Consciousness
or recitation, feel this internal vibrational frequency of light
have its positive effects: cleansing, healing, liberating, the surrender,
forgiveness, acceptance, tranquillity, and peace. Speak this awakening
influence from the heart to anyone You encounter during the day. Make
it Your primary energy source for Your Life, thus treating Yourself
and all the Human Beings as Divine Beings. Show the World
what is possible when We act as Awakened Consciousness.

The benefit of acting on Our highest excitement,
on this divine commitment & dedication, is that it
brings forth a **Society of Spiritual Intelligence**.

Coming from such a state of deep appreciation for the blessing
of being, as the Soul's True nature beyond the reasoning of the
mind, We are expressing Universal Wisdom on Earth. That is Our
ultimate purpose for sharing the Community as biological Beings.
Every Human is already doing Their best at any particular
moment and stage of Life. We can be that one more inspiration
on Their journey to enrol into Liberating Prominence collectively

L**ight**

Let's go back to the start and consider the most known Awakened
Teachers, thus acknowledging Jesus, Buddha, and Ramana,
for We'll need Their Inspiration to abide in the Light.
We'll need All Their Wisdom & Love, all the Peace!
What We see outside in the World is Our reminders to Abide in
Our Peace, Love, and Blessings, the Same Ones They Found Within.

*"The discovery that peace, happiness and love are ever-present within our own Being,
and completely available at every moment of experience, under all conditions, is
the most important discovery that anyone can make."* **Rupert Spira**

Love doesn't have a name, shape, or form, just like Light and just like
Consciousness, they are Universal, Free & All-encompassing.
WE ARE IT !

*Don't let the World define You, define Yourself according to
the innermost guidance: a Universal principle written in Light.*

The answers to any of Life's questions are not waiting out there in libraries,
churches, universities, scientific research centres, classrooms, inside the
minds & wisdom of gurus, or anywhere else far away in the Universe.
That is not the way the Universe, God, or Life work.

The Universe, God, and Life work in the way whereby You can
Only find All the answers, Here & Always, in Consciousness.
Consciousness is the Only Always & Ever-present Truth!
Therefore, there are no external truths.
All Truth Is Kept, and You can Find it Within Your Own Light!

Create Your own sacred space at home from the heart. Make it resonate
with the deepest sense of beauty, love, & peace that You are. Let this space,
this altar, garden, meditation, or prayer room be the one holiest centre to
Your graceful being, thus inspiring You to honour that God-Self essence

throughout the day. That atmosphere of inner peace is already the reason why We go to churches, mosques, temples, ashrams, spiritual retreats, or renewals. Keep that space free of daily occupations & obligations. That is where You rest in the inner Home of Light. That is how it feels to be in the presence of God – Your undisturbed Consciousness. By devoting to this shrine of One's Heart, You will never walk alone; You'll walk as Light. You will never be alone; You will be the presence of God.

Enlightening is the Light, to feel so light like the Light!

Your Awareness can be perceived as the Aliveness of Your Soul. It's Relaxing and it feels Free & Open, or Empty but Full of Existence. It is a heartfelt embrace of the softest grace, a beautiful, cheerful smile of pure undulated joy – non-resistance. It's Compassion, a deep-felt kindness for all Beings and all the Existence. It is Dedicating Yourself completely to Your partner, family, and friends, helping Those in need; staying in the mercy of Unconditional Love; & Feeling The World Deeply!

It is to lighten up a load of heavy mind thoughts. It is melting into the surroundings, into Beingness, and losing all & every sense of the imaginary self. It is a sheading of all the ego skin and becoming a New-born Soul of Light, the Light Itself!

Enlightenment is not like anything. It Is The Light! It is the most Beautiful Morning and the most Romantic Sunset. It is the most Wonderful of Days, every day, every moment!

Feeling the warmth of the SUN on Your closed eyes, that Orange-Yellow, Photon-Essence Enlightening Sensation is the Single closest image and feeling that can describe LIGHT

* * *

To LIFE! Thank You! Thank You! Thank You

Jesus

The Most Influential Being In Human History!

His Life & Teachings are the most Familiar, the most Intimate, and
the most Personal example of Living Unconditionally as the Awakened
Awareness that Shines the Light of Consciousness out Unto The World.

He is the Personification of Our Life's Journey on Earth, presenting
Us with Purity of Being, Awakening, and Service to Humanity.

Jesus Taught Us always to stay contemplative, to be fully Conscious
and, with that, to also allow the cessation of separation as Unconditional
Love. He is said: *"Thou shalt love the Lord thy God with all thy heart, and with
all thy soul, and with all thy mind. Thou shalt love thy neighbour as thyself."*
It is in the observation of Flowers that We can notice how peaceful they
are, thus abiding in their natural state, which when applied to Us refers
to the state of no-mind, of seeing reality as it is, which, before the fall
& the separation has always been thought of as being an undeniable
The Kingdom of Heaven on Earth for both Nature and Humans.

Jesus teaches Us to remember who We are in the broadest sense,
outside of Civilisation, as Spirit, as Soul, inhabiting this sacred vehicle
We call the body, and that upon freeing Ourselves from the ego, We'll
sit Right next to God! Jesus is the Pure Enlightened Presence
and the most Direct, Closest Son of God!

With Us being Their Children

*   *   *

*"I AM With You Always,
Even Unto The End
of The World..."*

<u>Devotion</u>

When We meet, know, and feel Jesus as the embodiment of
unconditional love & Consciousness, His statements such as,
*"I am the way and the truth and the life, no one comes to the Father except
through me"*, will be understood in the real light of their true meaning.

We can not directly find liberation in the worship of gurus or Gods but
in the authenticity of One's own realisation as Consciousness that IS.
This doesn't mean religious or spiritual devotion is wrong and
that We shouldn't practice it. On the contrary, it is encouraged
(I myself am a devotee and a humble servant of God's many
manifestations), but know that, as The Self that You Are, devotion
is only a doorway to God. Remember that tHere is no God, God IS!

Still, language & vocalizations, symbols & imagery are powerful
influences & inspirations for Awakening. We use countless prayers,
mantras, chants, recitations, songs, and movies to connect with
the divine inside. *Let Your prayers be a Thankful Affirmation for the
Gift of Life We have, and for the Healing We're always receiving.*

Here are the most famous examples, starting with Jesus's prayer:
*Our Father, who art in heaven, hallowed be thy name; thy kingdom come;
thy will be done on earth as it is in heaven. Give us this day our daily bread;
and forgive us our trespasses as we forgive those who trespass against us;
and lead us not into temptation, but deliver us from evil. Amen.*

Heart-touching melodies of *Amazing Grace*, Handel's *Hallelujah*,
Bach's *Air on the G string*, and Schubert's *Ave Maria*.

From eastern traditions there are the transcendent chants:
-*Aum* or *the Om*. -*Ohm shanti shanti shanti*. -*Om Namah Shivaya.*
-*Hare Krishna, Hare Krishna, Krishna Krishna, Hare Hare.*
Hare Rama, Hare Rama, Rama Rama, Hare Hare.
-*Om mani padme hum.*
-*Namu Myoho Renge Kyo*

Buddha

Siddhartha Gautama, the Awakened One!

As the story goes He was born to a King. But after enjoying
all the comforts of palace Life, and upon realising how Ageing,
Sickness and Dying are integral and inevitable parts of Everyone's
Life experience, He left His Wife and Child in the Search to
End Suffering. The End to the Karmic cycle of Birth & Death.

After Meditating for six years, He observed that all Suffering comes
from a Person's Dissatisfaction with Their Thoughts, Feelings, Sensations,
Perceptions as well as from The mind's addictive Attachments to Desire,
Wanting, and Craving. But by practising certain Virtues in Life and staying
Present, One can disassociate from this conditioned imaginary sense of
self, or ego, and Abide In Everlasting Wisdom, Peace, and Nirvana,
which come as a result of this Self-realisation.

To find the Buddha, all You have to do is See Your Nature.

Upon Centring Himself in The Middle Way, as That prior to all
thoughts I AM Recognition; The Knowing of One's True nature,
He remained a Conscious Witness, He got Enlightened!

Continually Teaching Wisdom of the Noble Eightfold Path:
Right Understanding, Right Thought, Right Speech, Right Action,
Right Livelihood, Right Effort, Right Mindfulness and
Right Concentration; the Core Truth of ThySelf,
The Pure Consciousness

*   *   *

"Do not dwell in the past, do not dream of the future,
concentrate the mind on the present moment."

Wisdom

An utmost presence sets me down like the weight of Awareness, which weighs infinitely nothing. Its gaze pierces the World and sets it free of time, where Existence collapses into the point of Consciousness.

One could exclaim from the fearless, freeness joy, but the Seer keeps a watchful eye, absent of thought, in the silent celebration, with God as a sight, and God inside, closer to the Truth than truth, truer than true.

While sitting still he closes the energy field, circulates the chi, spins the chakras, amplifies the aura, brightens the halo, travels the astral body, encourages a heart-talk, channels the higher self, brings forth the Soul, elicits in Spirit, and rests in God.

What is it that knows the Seer; who is it, how is it, why is
it, for how long it is? Being Yourself or being the Self?
By seeing the World as it Is, there is no World;
there is only IS. That is the Seer!

In wanting nothing from Anyone,
he gets everything from Everyone.
In thinking nothing, he has thought of everything.
In dreaming nothing, he lives the dream.

A weary Seer cushions dreams in awareness
and softens sleep by advocating prayers.

With a settled mind, he travels motionless;
with the aware breath, abides omnipresent;
with an unwavering stare, stands omnipotent;
with the wisdom of not knowing, sleeps omniscient.

Blanket Yourself with the warming Sun that bolsters
Your presence for the calming night.

When the night of day becomes darker than the dark of the night, the baggage of a personal story weighs unbearably on the dreamer.

He is gridlocked in dreadful sighs of anxiety measured by the shortness of breath and the entire prospect of Life comes fully crashing down; a hopeless individual can only see comfort in the sudden, premature death of much-needed end:

How does a Man bear the weight of Existence,
How does it live, and how does it die.
What is One's right path, the true destiny?

Do We act upon Our passions or stay as abiding peace?
And both could bring bliss, and both are a mirror of another.

How do We awaken the sleeping beauty, filled with treasures
of Consciousness, or do We transcend the transcendence?

There is tremendous loneliness here, broken by the bursts
of laughter, receding into the gridlock of suffering again.

Once more, this is yet another escape in avoiding a
writer's suicide, that comforting promise of ending in
literate paradise. So farewell until We get another
glimpse of the shining light of the Sun.

But as We look anew into the essence of sorrow through
Our loving Souls, the joy of being is shining ever so vividly.

This image of the ghostly past is a desperate attempt
to glimpse the former glory of the awakened Self.

How pitiful has the search become, how empty, so
dull, that We can't recognise even the single moment
of the truth that is right in front and already inside?

By the truth that he is, Those in anguish are drawn to him.
Fearing that fact, They seek comfort in lies but They will
forever tremble at his sight, quiver from hearing his voice,
shake by his touch, and speak of rumours in trepidation.

Now softened by his appeasement, They turn and are won over
when called & approached, reconciled with his unwavering support.
The poor pilgrims are left bespoken as reawakened for the cause.
One can truly be without addiction; it's as simple as having
no attachments and breaking all habits.

*All You have to do is stay in the Sun all day and
all night, then the light of Consciousness will freely shine.*

The honesty of One's solitude, the serenity of Your seclusion and
the decency of having integrity purify Your heart with a joyful smile.

The Knower is adamant about continuing and stops at nothing short
of a miracle. He manifests jewels for pious seekers, saintly monks,
religious venerates, spiritual devotees, fanatic fundamentalists,
an unruly mob, free spirits, hippies, doubters, ordinaries,
regulars, commoners, every-days, and just nobodies.

*In His penetrating Look, his unprecedented Stare,
AWAKENING is felt in the Transcendence of his Gaze.*

He only sees beauty in Humanity and how all is well;
having no polarised opinion, no agenda, no expectation,
no error, he remains in grace without ever straying away.

His Awareness is unaffected by observers, his gaze is undeterred
neither by principality nor power. His stare is his courage, his pose a
mighty stature, as he conquers with divine presence, and assimilates
through condolences, he captures Their Hearts by leaving Them be.

The entire history of the World and the whole span of Existence

flashes between the rise & fall of each & every breath. It gets
recognised in an utmost serenity, in the space of a single Now.

Ohh, how greatly I felt the moment I saw You,
in the Presence of Divine Truth, I knew I have come to.

A tremendous light of relaxation comes from the certainty in
the current state of being, liberating an unexpected character, an
unsuspected victim, as it brings forth the spectator from a passenger
seat right to the very front, in the most natural of states as an
observance of itself. It frees One from conceptualised bondage and
frees You from bewilderment. The Centre disappears in a breath
yet it burns as the light that shines with the infinitude of Suns.

He washes in the Sunshine and ignites the inner flame;
by opening a holy way, he shuts away Our pain.

A blazing inferno within, without an outside fuse,
illuminates itself with itself, like a candle onto a flame,
without wax, without fuel, shining by its very own light.

When Your day, week, or month turns into a haphazard mess, he
clarifies the problems and clears the drama, leaving You troubleless.

When Life feels like a lost cause, like a broken game, be sure to break
away from the chains, take Your stand, and make it one of grace.

He encloses You with love, encapsulates You in peace, lobotomises the
ego, paralyzes the mind, returns You to senses by staying as Awareness.

By making You concentrate on the present task, He makes You fall in
love at first sight, gives no need for a second glance or afterthoughts.
Focusing on determination solidifies You in a motionless sway:

*One begins by sitting down and saying nothing, stating nothing, and
claiming no thing. That is a good place, the best start and pose, to begin with.*

By freeing Oneself from Yourself, One frees himself from Everyone else,
and in so doing, He holds Them closer than He holds his own Dear Ones.

If the One feels great, then every hungry mouth, every homeless person,
every broken heart, every beaten wife, every bullied child, every tortured
animal, every waiting Soul can feel at least so good that it can feel
like being the part of it all, and can remain in peace at last.

Receive by keeping nothing but by giving everything.
Rejoice in the solitude of having the company of all
people in the World and all Beings in the Universe.

He is familiar with universality, infinity, presence of
sanity, general ambiguity, and overall understanding.
What has been foreshadowed is now foretold.

Love is a freed mind, a livelihood of a Soul;
it is One's most authentic True Self.
Spirit is the Life Energy of a God.
God is the Conscious Universe,
and in Consciousness, it Is All.

Find the truth in knowing not,
bring the abundance in having non.
Have the fulfilment in wanting nil,
open all doors by closing an ill.

Whichever modulation of manifestation
as the universal incarnation presents to him
and Whosoever he encounters crossing his path
is greeted by the very welcoming presence of God.

He will rendezvous with the lost and catalyse compassion,
striving to bring about inherent peace in Everyone, thus,
contributing to Humanity's general wellbeing.

By taking the trouble of going through hardship
to meet a friend, he will always endure, never
jeopardising the fellowship and he'll never meet the end.

Dead serious but laughingly concentrated and enveloped
with such a familiar relaxed presence, he never clenches a fist,
rather gestures with fingers and caresses the air with His palms.

He's been called many names yet remains unaccounted for,
unfamiliar but known, unrecognised, even famous
but celebrated and wide-worshiped as the light to Us all.

He foresees fluctuation, anticipates desire, and overcomes temptation,
even when allure backfires with emulation. He patiently answers in all
honesty formulated questions, postulates them by affirmation; rewards.

He doesn't support both sides, he knows only the Oneness of the game,
but he does inspire a will to live and encourages the opportunity to be.

He sees eternity in a crystal-clear sphere, where others see a tiny
drop of water – where others see a speck, he feels a shining space
so gently falling and awakening a humbling of grace.

He elevates in joy but humbles in pride.
He doesn't need Anyone's love, yet he loves Everyone.

He plants a seed of haste and studies it watchfully for
the whole century, thus escaping the circle of incarnation
that no longer infuses him in the World of domination.

He permeates throughout Existence by not taking a step,
by not breaking a sweat, and not overlooking a breath.

He concentrates all efforts on having no effort at all and
rearranges temples of sorrow, deciphering the writing on the wall.

He penetrates an ego by lifting the illusion of a veil,
and in abandoning the search, he will never search again.

He uplifts One's Spirit by the manner in which he breathes
and consumes the existential pain of all that can flee.

He harmonises the atmosphere when entering the room,
and with his eloquence, he embraces all that is due.

He strengthens a character by awakening the Soul,
which smiles in ecstasy from everything it knows.

He energises a neglected body with a potency of health
and heals psychic wounds while fasting from physical wealth.

He is swimming in the desert, bathing in the sand, and walks
weightlessly, from the lowest mountain to the highest valley.
He speaks wordlessly, sings voicelessly, and screams silently.

His eyes are flickering gems filled with bhakti love,
reflecting a divine of Being, and relinquishing the thoughts:

Investigate what remains when a thought goes away.
What is the primary aspect in all the experience?
What endures all passings? What outlasts all wanderings?
Consciousness is the term that We use to describe the Presence that
remains when a moving mind settles, from the disappearance of all else.
Meditation is the calming with which We experience Peace
and the transcendence of Awareness,
That prime Beingness is the Substratum of Existence !

A timeless moment of eternal silence
Non-existence of being infinite
Creation and destruction of every Now
Birthing and dying forever
The background noise in Awareness

The constancy of mind chatter
The illusion of being the thinker
Imagined chronological pain
A space where a thought goes away
Torment & torture of fear of going to waste
Surrender to non-resistance of the moment
The centre is shining with the joy of belonging
Opening a channel to inner wisdom
The warmth of an open heart
Deep breath in, long breath out
The conscious rhythm of the breath
Inevitable return to silence
A gesture of friendship, the grace of unconditional love
The re-emergence of the will
Certainty of being aware
Freedom of conscious stare
The magnificence of being awake
Free Your Self from yourself, settle as the abiding grace
Be in Nature, be as Nature
Speaking of Nature, whispering of being
Be the light that shines with the warmth of the Sun
Always remember to stay in the Sun, to feel the Source of Life
Only in Love can Life blossom. Only in the Now can Life Be
Be present then, be the ground of all being
It is a constant practice of staying true to Yourself: Consciousness
The decency of being Your integrity based on that
Go with Your Soul instinct, be what You want, live how You choose
If it means abandoning all traditional ways of interaction, so be it
The price is a thought, the prize is authenticity
Be the poet, artist, woodsmen, Wiseman; the Sage

All the miracles of creation infatuate him as he stands alone
by going the distance, by going strong. Powered by the flames
of freedom fire, which purifies the body and centres the mind,
he stays at peace, contented that he forgets, for there's nothing to
forgive, or remember, nor does he hold on to the grave.

He was birthed in a promise and born in timeless hope;
he grows in perseverance of the Life-affirming bliss.

He reawakens the senses by decomposing the stress and
re-emerging in devotional glory like a canonised Saint.

He excels at beingness but contemplates getting old, in
the stare of the Now, fear of dying young thus he overcomes.

He makes friends with the animals and tends to them with care so
that in his loving embrace they themselves become self-aware.

Because of such Life that he incarnates, the Life of holy silence,
he can't even function and can't even speak; he is the Sage.

He is described as Sacred, and he's been called Divine;
They gave him the title Sri, meaning nectar so Supreme.

Those who flock to see him for the miracles he brings,
'ooh' in wordless utterance, delights Our dearest Seer.

He brings out the significance of joy, a glimpse of an
awakened self. As Bhagavan he is known to most, so
gracious, Self-abiding, and a heartily welcoming host.

If You could feel his magnanimous stare,
You would know of his Presence,
for You have seen it in his gaze,
Ramana Maharshi is his very name

*   *   *

"All that is required to realise the Self is to Be Still.

Let what comes come. Let what goes go. Find out what remains."

Ramana

Bhagavan Sri Ramana Maharshi, The Sage of Arunachala!

Arguably the most Aware Human We know and have footage of!

Growing up in South India, at 16, He went through a profound
Self-realisation, which sent Him to seek The Holy Arunachala Hill.
After Feeling the Mountain as God Thyself, He Abided there,
Immersed in Stillness, in the State Beyond Mind and Time,
for the Rest of His Life, despite writing little and barely
speaking, attracting thousands who witnessed:

Personality & Character of Perfection, The Great Seer,
Divine Gaze, A Sight of God, The Liberated Being!

"He never wanted anything from anyone." He never showed a
difference between classes of People or even Animals,
who responded to His Presence with Intelligence.

His Teachings on Self-enquiry comprise the Most
Direct Path on Liberation from the false self. But His
Greatest Inspirations were those Contemplated,
Illuminated, Enlightened, Self-realised,

in SILENCE

*   *   *

*"They say that I Am dying! But I'm not going away.
Where could I go? It is the body that dies...*

I AM HERE"

"Ocean of Nectar, Full of Grace,
Engulfing the Universe in Thy Splendour!
Oh, Arunachala – the Supreme Itself!
Be Thou the Sun, and open the Lotus of my Heart in Bliss."

The timeless Being is the Sun eternal, streaming ceaselessly as Awareness,
flowing effortlessly as Abidance. It is the present kind-heartedness
and a flourishing beauty of the One Beloved

Silence

Language is a means to communicate and express within advanced social Life forms. How & when did language develop as opposed to appearance of thoughts, or did they arise simultaneously? Do tribal people have thoughts, or do They live in a constant presence? Is Human intelligence a product of such linguistical and mindful evolution?

If examined closely, language is a verbal expression of the deeper understanding – inner knowing. The only way You can know what the Other person is communicating to You is if You've experienced such knowledge Yourself. In other words, if You have personal and unquestionable experience of what They are trying to communicate, You will understand Them.

For example, Love can symbolise many feelings & meanings, or God. But how do We know what We mean when using such broad concepts? Of course, We know everything about Love & God. We're surrounded by endless stories, movies, songs, books, teachings, and preaching's – such a vast variety of information. But how can We determine what is True and can We claim the definitive knowledge of Love, God, or any concept of Human language?
Language is a Spell, a Signpost, a Symbol for the experience.
And all these experiences are ones of the limited selves. Of the mind, thoughts, feelings, sensations. All changing, flittering, temporary.

Language is an artificial construct; the Vocal Game on top of a Silent Existence. It could never truly represent the Ultimate Truth, so We should seek The Truth in the domain of Stillness: Silence. In that deeper dimension of Knowing Our Being!

But We're too uncomfortable with Silence. We're constantly seeking the next thing that will distract Us from being Still, so We end up speaking just to break this unease with Silence. This addiction to avoiding Silence is responsible for most of the noise in the World.

By following Your breath, notice the constant aliveness within the body. Listen to that Silence and feel how there is a deep and an eternal pleasant stillness that underlies all of Life. Observe the empty room without the need to add anything to it. Look outside at the moving tree branches, witness the wind's effect without hearing the sound. Watch the World with that underlying emptiness, the base upon which all sound and action happens.

Consciousness, Peace, Awareness, Beingness, Wakefulness, Alertness!

These terms, again, only point to a specific type of experience, to the Knowing Within Ourselves. Basically, they are merely words, just a language suggesting the type of experience.

We must go beyond words, beyond language, beyond mind, and thoughts to experience something that lies outside of those attributes of Human perception. We must Abide by Inner Peace and Be the Pure Consciousness to Be, and therefore Know, That which is Unexplainable.

Only Silence can express the Divine Love that every Soul Is. No words can truly touch the eternal realm of Spirit. Silence is the Conscious recognition of the Sacred Oneness of Existence. A Silence is the true Soul talk, the holiest acknowledgment of Source. That is why God is eternally silent, for it can't be otherwise. Everything that speaks is not coming from God but separation, yearning to return to God. God is Consciousness; Consciousness is Silence. To be Silent is to honour God in Yourself and Others, as in Namaste greeting.

"Whatever is destined not to happen will not happen, try as you may. Whatever is destined to happen will happen, do what you may to prevent it. This is certain. The best course, therefore, is to remain silent."
Ramana Maharshi

The only True Language of the Absolute Truth, is then to be found in the Silent Awareness

Awareness

We are all victims of The World and that manifests as ego,
but it is in the nature of Ourselves to return to the normalcy
of One's True self, as the presence of Awareness. The joy of
not holding on to thoughts or identity is the state of bliss –
the true freedom – freedom from being besieged by thoughts,
from the constant bombardment of mind commentaries,
from the illness of involuntary self-talk, and
mad actions on ego's behalf.

Why be a home without a host, a forest with no trees,
harvest without a crop, a rock without solidity, air that is not empty,
a bird that can't fly with wings that are tied, laughter without a smile,
eyes with no tears of bliss, a heart without love, pain with no sorrow,
a morning without Sun, a child with no family, or parents without children,
grass with no soil, plant without flowers, touch with no care,
Sun without warmth, Life with no hope, Sea without fish,
a Planet with no Beings, a meal without food, a drink with no liquid,
crying without tears, book without pages, library with no books,
handshake with no hands, house on drifting sand,
ignorance without shame, suspect with freedom, trapped outside
prison, sentenced with no bars, statue with no face, rule without a law,
government without blame, bankrupt like a state?

Don't poison Your Heart with jealousy, don't close Your mind
with attachments, rather, quite the opposite. Be joyful for Others'
happiness, be delighted for Their progress & success, make Their
satisfaction the primary goal of Your Life, in Your own way.

It can be the best partner & parent, being true throughout
any job, action, duty, or responsibility One is performing.
Taking care of the environment or Those in need, developing
sustainable technology, or remaining in peace, and not polluting
the World with the heavy energy of ego's indulgences.

With melting into a lightness of being, You're flowing in the heart's intuition. *"Abiding as the Self in unalloyed happiness."*

Why not be the sound without noise, shape with no form,
a ship that can't sink, sunshine without clouds, worriless mind,
stressless time, sleep with no dreams, free like Nature,
open like an Ocean, empty like air, caring like compassion,
wise like sage, kind like grandparents, carefree like a child,
contended like a monk, graceful like Saint,
cleansing like water, healing like herbs, singing like a bird,
sleeping like a bear, and Awakening of the supreme Self?

Be a supreme state of presence where nothing that happens
in the Universe can take You out of Your serene tranquility.
Not the death of loved ones or even the death of the World.
Not even the death of the Universe and not even One's own death.
It is literally a state of no thoughts, no reasoning, no resistance,
no distinctions of Self or Others, but a harmony of perceptions.

Once You surrender to the Ocean of being still, immersed in
a tide of presence, float on the waves of unspoken wisdom,
devoted only to the moment, the urgency, primacy,
and constancy of Awareness. **The Self of all selves***:*

Whatever experience You are Aware of is not who You are.
Who is Aware of an experience, thoughts and feelings?
Who is Aware? The Awareness Itself!

The only truth there is to any
experience is the Awareness of it.
Without Awareness, there would be no experience.
Yet without experience, there is only Awareness.
Only Awareness can be aware of the experience.
Only Awareness can be aware.

Awareness doesn't need the experience to know Itself.
Experience needs Awareness for the experience to be known.

Only Awareness can be aware of Itself.
Only Awareness can know Awareness!

Awareness is the constant stream of Awareness.
It is never changing; it is never absent.
All experience appears within this stream of Being.
All experience is experienced within Awareness.
Awareness can never be absent from the experience.
But experience is always absent from Awareness.
Awareness is the absence of all experience!

To be fully aware means to be free from experience.
To be free from experience implies full Awareness.
Awareness is never lost to Itself.
Awareness is always fully aware of Itself.
Awareness is aware of Itself, as Awareness.
Awareness can only be aware of Itself,
as the Awareness of Itself.

All experience arises and recedes in Awareness.
Awareness must be here always for the experience to occur.
Nothing ever happens outside Awareness.
Everything happens within Awareness.

Awareness is the only constant that never happens.
Yet everything happens in the constancy of Awareness!

"Abide in Awareness with no illusion of person.
You will be instantly free and at peace." **Ashtavakra Gita**

Awareness is the subjective truth to all experiences.
Experience is the objective truth in Awareness.
An experience is an object of the subject.
An object is an experience of the subject.

A subject is experienced in Awareness as an object.
The subject of experience is an object.
An object is an experience within Awareness.
The sense of I is the experience in Awareness.
Awareness is never the experience of the I.

I is the objective experience of subjective Awareness,
wherein the subject of experience is Awareness of I.
To be fully aware is an Awareness of the subject.
Thus, I, as an experience, never arises in the subject.
To subject Yourself to experience, as an object,
brings forth the Awareness of the objective subject.

Awareness is the subject of all experience.
Experience is always Awareness of the subject.
The subject is the Awareness of an object.
An object is being aware within the subject.
Experience in the subject is an object.
Experience of the object is in the subject.
An object is subjected in Awareness.

AWARENESS IS

*   *   *

"Awareness isn't something we own; awareness isn't something we possess.
Awareness is actually what we are." **Adyashanti**

Meditation

Being aware as Awareness, Attentive of the Now,
is what Meditation is, the Pure Presence of Awareness.

If Prayer is a Conversation with God, Meditation is Peace with God.
It is the Life of Consciousness, as the Attention of Awareness.

Finding that perfect body position where We can remain
fully relaxed and centred as Awareness is the entry point
into Meditation. Then the Peace of God is Peace in Us.

Meditation is the ultimate magic of the Universe,
as it is the greatest statement of the Self-aware Beings.

Meditation is a sacred practice of Abiding in One's Being
until the practice becomes effortless, which is where it ceases
to be practice and ceases to be meditation. It becomes
an effortless activity and Is the Pure Consciousness.

Meditation must become the single most important
practice and technique of any Conscious Being.
It must be as essential to Them as the Sun is to Life.

*Meditation is the most unnatural behaviour for the
mind, but it is the very Nature of Consciousness.*

Meditation means to contemplate thoughts.
In other words, it is to be aware of whatever
arises within the body/mind perception.

It is the very Awareness of the objective experience.
It's the recognition that the subject itself is in Awareness,
and within that, letting go of the sense of separation,
thus, allows glimpses of Liberation

Enlightenment

Enlightenment is Staying in the Constant Quality of Being Aware!
Relaxed In – Centred Out. It is the Focus of Staying Present,
Intent on Being Completely Still, Non-resistant to What Is.

You neither accept, nor do You not accept. You Observe
as it Is. Looking with No One behind the observation;
It is The Looking Itself. Eternal Gaze, Infinite Knowing,
Present Moment, Stillness. The Continuous State of Being Awake!

It is the Ever-present Observation, where One Sees that only
mind & body ever change while everything else stays the same.

It is like running around the World, chasing happiness,
searching for love, to then find it back home, as Yourself.

It is to have a photographic memory and remember every
detail, to never forget anyone or anything that ever happened,
yet still leaving them behind, immediately & constantly.

It means nothing will move You. You won't react
or feed into the stream of thoughts and events.
Nothing disturbs You, and nothing forces You.

It is the reason Everyone will leave You and You
will stay completely alone, since Their minds can't accept
something They don't experience or know for Themselves.

But if They recognise the Truth of Your Silence, and Your
Unconditional Wisdom, They could accept You yet in
the glimpses of pauses and brain freezes You triggered.

It doesn't mean You are always happy. It means You are beyond
the experiencing. You Know, You See, You Stay as You Are.

Enlightenment for the mind is to see Yourself as everything.
But for Your Being is to Know Yourself as Nothing.

It is when the mind declares himself a God, yet You remain as a Plant or a Rock. It is when one group calls You messiah, guru, teacher, while another group puts You into a mental hospital and behind bars, yet You Remain Constant, Loving, Present.

Awakening is to be Yourself as Yourself!
It is to Never separate Yourself from the Stream of Gazing.
To never move Your eyeballs, to never blink, and never sleep.

It is to be Saint as Seer. Magician as Shaman.
Lover to Self, Grace to Others.

It is to Arrive on Time precisely when You mean to,
even if Everyone else is running late. It is an Eternal Crucifixion
and Never-ending Last Supper. It's the Smile of a Child, and
the Gaze of a Sage. It is the Dawn and Set. It is the SUN Itself!

It's to Never Want, Desire, or Crave, because You already
have Everything and You found it by having Nothing.

It is to be Alpha & Omega, both Male & Female.
It is the Beginning, End, and Everything in Between.

It is to work and never complain. It is to never Start
because You've already Finished.

It is to paint a Masterpiece but to leave the canvas Empty
and to Build the Cathedral but leave the stones Unmoved.

It is to Sculpt a David, leaving the rock Uncarved, to Slay the
Dragon or Kill Goliath, while leaving the Beasts Alive.
Image Untouched, Object Unrealised!

It is to Be Able To, but never Move a Mountain.
It is to Sing a Universal Opera, even if You can't utter
a sentence or can't even raise Your voice.

It is to write a Bible for every kind, even if You are entirely illiterate.

Awakening will make You Omniscient, Omnipresent, Omnipotent,
and, yet, You will sit on a Park Bench and take no pride or part in it.

You will be World famous, even if nobody has ever known or seen You.
It will offer a feast of all pleasures, yet You will start fasting.
You will be tempted but You'll take no prize
because You'll Recognise Yourself as the tempter Itself.

So, it's never to bite Your lip or move Your eyes,
neither think a thought, nor be Your mind.
To never go astray, to always simply stay.

It's to pledge guilt even if the fault is not Yours.
To beg Your pardon and wisely catch Yourself.

I Am Awakened, yet nobody is There.
You are Awakened too, but You always move away.

Enlightenment Is Perceiving Reality As It Is. The Perceiving Itself.

It is the Absence of the Person, Presence of the Seer.
There is no Me or You, there is only one answer to Who Am I?
There is only I AM

*　　*　　*

*"To know yourself as the Being underneath the thinker, the stillness
underneath the mental noise, the love and joy underneath the pain,
is freedom, salvation, enlightenment."* **Eckhart Tolle**

True Freedom

Freedom! Ah, the Goodness of Being!
Wearing Uplifting, Healing Sun Rays as a Smile.
No Thoughts, just Observing, Thanking for Existence.

I Am Free; my Mind is Open, my Heart is Pure, my Body is Healthy!

There is nothing You need to do other than be Yourself.
Just to Breathe is Enough to Be, to Abide in Your Being.

"You need nothing to be happy - you need something to be sad." **Mooji**

The ego wants something since it is not at peace; it is restlessness because the ego is lacking. While Consciousness is peace, it wants nothing, so it asks for nothing. Cut the minds attachments (ego) to all and every desire, wanting, or craving, and You will be free. You will be free of the World, of time, and space. You will abide in One's authentic Self, which is the peace of being present. You as Consciousness will be One with the joyful Heart.
Your body & mind will then be an instrument of God.

This state of being knows no fear. It lets go of thoughts and creates no negativity. It is One with totality as it makes no separations. Such freedom from the mind and experience of Oneness manifests as a gentle smile and the penetrating look of eternal radiance. All this may sound extraordinary, but it is Everyone's True nature. It's the simplest & foremost state, but the one hardest to retain due to the incessant activity of the mind. Another pointer towards being such presence is to combine the attention with the fullness of One's breath (where each is acknowledged and followed), with the joyousness of the heart, and an unbroken graceful stare. *This state is all together, therefore, it is as light as God's very own Light.*

As You stay in Your authentic feeling of bliss, You will know what every teacher throughout history has spoken about. You will know They have taught from Their own state of bliss which is the joy of a liberated heart.

Gandhi said, *"Happiness is when what You think, say, and do are in harmony."*
And on an external level, that is true, as in staying true to Your character.
But in Self-inquiry, We must go deeper and notice how the true happiness
of joy is freedom from thoughts, which ultimately frees You from feeling
and doing in accordance with identifying with thoughts. So Descartes's
proclamation, *I think, therefore I am*, is too, only interesting on an outer level.
For in the absence of thoughts, there won't be anything other than I Am.
Or to be precise, Amness of Being. Most people think They have found
freedom in being Themselves, but They are playing the mind's script.
And the play may be a pleasant one, as satisfying Your ego tend to be.
The World is set at such a fast pace that One never has time to ask Oneself
Who is enjoying or suffering? *Who am I?* Upon enquiring on such essential
questions, We are due to realise *I am That*, which knows the freedom of not
needing to ask another question and the freedom of not needing to know
another answer. People are afraid of losing everything by leaving
everything, not knowing that only in having nothing lies True Freedom.
In owning nothing, nothing can own You. Buddha, Jesus, and Ramana
lived free like that, as illuminating spiritual beauty of being the Light to
the World. When that indescribable feeling of peace & freedom hits You,
You won't be able to do anything other than abide motionless in it.

   You will be the silent witness. You will be THAT.

God lay in the ability to recognise the Uniqueness of each Moment.
Where Every NOW is the Best ONE!

Allow Yourself this Freedom from The World, and in that Space,
observe as things happen without the need to interpret them.
Then the Need for Right Action may Arise. Follow that
Intuition and act according to the Just Cause.
How Do You Know It? It Will Feel Right

   *   *   *

*Once You Awaken from Conditioning, Who You Are
and Why We Are Here, Will Be Remembered & Known*

CHAPTER 8

NATURE

Permaculture

We're all a reckless wreck from the Lost Civilisation,
indulging in the culture of classism and privatisation,
forgetting Our Natural roots in the quest for World domination,
cutting down the trunks of Trees and replacing them with
pillars dedicated to glorified Gods and monetary shrines.

Remember how long We have stood with aeons
and walked with winds & seasons for millennia!
Never have We gone against the currents, but
floated on the Oceans, swum with streams, grown
the best of seeds, gathered fruits, and composted
waste, to benefit from the tastes improved by
artificial selection of the Natural multiplication.

These are off-grid dreams of Permacultural reality
hereby of detox recovery, from an initial loss of sanity,
in the newfound freedom of Gaia's diversity.

Now Awakening the Soul-senses by laying on the
ground, keeping Our hands & feet in dirt & soil,
feeling the pulse of the Sun's glittering daylight, and
following night metronomes of distant starlight.

This dedication to living sustainably in wooden
houses, open terraces, with fairy artisan decorations
and wicker chairs facing the views of eternity,
mixed with scents of organic vegetable gardens,
where pets with no masters freely play, loses You
in the flames of night fires and healing seances,
which are lighting Fires in Our Hearts,
summoning an ancient language and
speaking the tongue of trees,
glorifying flowers, and bees

Fragrance

"There is a Wonderful Fragrance in the Air!"
An Ever-expanding Invitation into Formless Essence.
Where the Luminous Sunshine infiltrates the thinker, leaving him
dazzled, confused, and standing in Awe. In Awe I Said! Of the Natural
call to come back Home. To be as You Are, Infinite & Timeless.
To come back Home to Self, to Peace, as Light.

So hear me again, my Dears! You Are the Brilliance in disguise!
And once You strip Yourself Free from mind-made tendencies,
it's like Embarking on the Grand Mission of Laughter in Life!
The Constant Fascination with **Being, Blessing,** and **Healing!**
All that was neglected will Now be Honoured, will Thus be Cured.

And my, my oh my! How have We been so blind and afraid that
We couldn't differentiate the BIGGER picture, from the small !

And I don't ask for praise, nor do I ask for money. But I only seek of You,
to taste & feel, that it is not blood which pours out of Our mental wounds.
It is the Undulated Bliss, of this Soul-filtered Honey! Ha-ha!

So come, Drink with me from this Fountain of Joy, and don't forget to
remember To Be Yourself! It is in the Courage to Live as Your Feeling
Heart that makes Us dripping wet at the Source of Oneness, as Mana
flows in Heaven, from this Never-ending and Overflowing pitcher.

In the Enormity of Our Being's Gaze,
We Feel, We Perceive, a Wonderful Fragrance, in the Air

*   *   *

"Let's Kiss This Life Like It Were A Love Affair, & Every Being Our Beloved."
Dreaming-Bear Baraka Kanaan, Wild Love Kissed into Consciousness

Tripping like Heaven

Today, I was Tripping like Heaven!
Intoxicated by the Spirit of Nature Itself.
Its Only Side-effect, being Love, Left me
Hallucinating like a Crazed Lunatic on Source Essence,
Composing & Performing this Divine Rap of Sacred Heart.

This Miraculous and Elusive State We call Nirvana,
Enlightenment, Bliss, Authenticity, Realisation of True Self,
Illuminated me by the Shining Light of the Sun's Rays,
Penetrating every Pore of Body and Worry of Mind,
about what might happen at the End of Time.

Because this very state of Complete thoughtlessness
is doing Quantum Healing atom-sized jumps,
from One All-encompassing wavering Reality to another
Super Unified Graviton Vibrating Massage of Sweetly Ting-tingling
Holy Laughter, which in turn Honours Your Inner Child by
keeping Your Innocence Alive enough to See the Blissful
Oneness in Everyone and Everything in Existence,
Gracefully Floating as Magnificent Swans
and in Awe of those Heavenly Doves!

Now that You have had a glimpse of this Destined
Self, filled with Visions of what True Paradise is all about,
how can You refuse to come Dancing High, Joined in
Hands with Care intended Compassionate Gestures,
Gently Sharing a Free Hug of Forgiveness!

It's When We allow Ourselves to Be Wild & Free like This,
with no Intent other than being Original & Real, that All
this Flattering Goodness comes fully charging at the
doors of illusions, leaving Our insecurities & fears
to crash down the hallways of separation!

189

So choose Your authenticity, instead of spiritual emulation,
and all the blessedness of the Soul will surely come to fruition.

An Awakened mind: *cries the tears of Heaven, angelizes the Soul,*
collaborates, confronts, lets go, sacrifices, gives, gets, grows, warms,
accepts, kisses, hugs, loves, joins, celebrates, straightens, corrects,
exists, lingers, abides, returns, cares, satisfies, vibrates, beautifies,
stays, helps, encounters, welcomes, fills, nourishes, embodies, faces,
strives, comes up with, figures, moves swiftly, gently, graciously,
magnanimously, firmly, naturally, with dignity & grace, stems,
invigorates, calms, borns, dies, flies, hovers, heavenz, Godz!

What You find then is this Sweetly Sleeping
but Ascending, Awakening Being,
Flirtatiously Gossiping with Your Soul Essence,
Inviting You to the Bliss of the Moment
that The One Cannot Refuse Now,
and thus Arriving at Nothing

But To Join In
the
Awareness

*   *   *

Of Man & Nature, the Unison of Life!

Out Here in the Natural Vastness
exists the Primal State of Being.
By making a Natural Trip, You're
transcending physical-mental form,
You Venture outside Space-Time,
and by Witnessing this Exhilaration,
You're tapping into the Source.
Into the Beingness Thyself

Rise In Love

Yesterday I fell in Love again.
Or should I say, I Rose In Love!
The Same As I Do Every Day.

But this time was different, more intimate &
passionate, more vital & true. Stronger and More Alive!

I Saw how Your SUN was the Life-giving Light!

I Noticed how Your Soil is a Mirror of You,
showing Us how Your Deepening Roots
Spring out and Blossom as Incredible Trees.

I Saw how birds, insects, animals All interact,
benefit, and share in this Miracle of Creation.

This is the Love, the Equilibrium, the Symbiosis,
the Permaculture, the Equality of Nature Itself.
It's in this Phenomenon of Life that I found myself
Immersed. I Discovered it, I Felt it, I Sensed it.

Then, I Saw that Your Rivers are Vital Arteries of
this Freedom to Experience Life, with Mountains
& Rocks releasing the Essential Minerals, mixing
them with the Soil's Fundamental Nutrients,
allowing for this Feast of countless species to
happen under the Glowing SUN. Ooh God!

But then, You Left Us Amazed and Mystified, as We
would be at Wandering Stars while Gazing at the Night Sky,
full of Comet Tails, X Planets, and Hollow Moons, speckled
on the Backbone of the Milky Way's Shimmering Lights.

And so, what about Us? Who Are We in this Story on Earth?
Well, my Dears! You are the Brain, the Eye, the Feel,
and the Holy Witness behind it All.

For if there weren't Your Brilliant Existence as Human,
all this Sensation of Nature would have gone unnoticed.
That's How Important You Are!

You've been given the Royal Seat of Consciousness,
Looking, Observing, and Monitoring it All. And vice versa.

To extend Your Senses and Honour the Earth by Enveloping
Her Nature & Nurture, is to Abide as the Spirit,
Cherishing All the expressions of Life. For All
have come out of It and All will return to It.

That is God, to Abide in the Lasting Connection.
To not separate that which is One in Essence.

That is how every Tribe in the Wilderness Lives.
Outside preliminary thoughts, centred in the
actual day & night, morphogenesizing from the
current season, and cannibalising on real events.
And it's not a belief, rather, Feeling the Raw Reality.

Nature Speaks to You, like Silence, like Beauty, as
Motion without judgment, and as Divine Voice.
Teaching You, Remembering You, Showing You
That Who You Are and Who We Are
Is the Love, Is ONE

*   *   *

There is the Mother Earth of Senses,
right Beneath Your Feet

The Soundtrack of Nature

Today, again, I Spent an entire Day amongst Nature!

Benefitting from Her Eternal Presence and
listening to my favourite Transcending score:
THE SOUNDS OF NATURE !
Here, *"Nothing Is Written."* Here, Life Is!

*A Tree, a bird's song, and a flower will teach You more about
the Nature of Life than anything ever written or experienced
outside of it, if You allow Yourself to be As It Is.*

If saying Larger Than Life can truly be worthy,
then the Title goes to The Greatest and Most Expansive
Documentary ever made: MOTHER NATURE !

*To awaken Your Soul and become intimate with Nature,
and to be that Spark that ignites Flames of Freedom
in People's eyes, is to be in Love with Life.*

My fascination with Her endless entertainment is
creating a new genre of Archaeological storytelling,
which furthermore, Wins an Award for the best
Original Music and Sound effects.

Never did some Musical Score
Compliment a Documentary so Naturally,
so Majestically, so Theatrically, so Emotionally,
so Dramatically, Mysteriously, and Magnificently!

All in all, it's a Time Travel Saga which will take
Your mind and Soul across the Spends of millennia,
where You'll face Your own mortality of this mere
few thousand years of Human Civilisation.

What You now see as Nature, took countless ages to form.
The cliché is saying millions of years but do You
understand and believe that such a claim is a fact?
Where does that knowing take Your intellect, Your Soul?

These realisations show that even though there are
fascinating Man-made structures in the World, which are
awe-inspiring in themselves, the Natural World around
You is infinitely more ancient, older, and Alive!

And We, Conscious Beings, are Here Now,
occupying this Vast Natural World.
Here, just for a few recorded millennia.

And You Individual Human, for just a few
fleeting decades, in the Eternity of Space.

So in these uncertain times, when
We all face the prospect of death and loss,
what better meditation than to align Yourself
with that which is immortal in essence:
Nature,

The Spirit of Life Itself

*   *   *

The eternal silence and constant buzz, slow growth.
Flowering beauty, death in an instant, and immediate birth.

Fresh air and the wind blows, a hurricane drops.
Vast destruction and steady absorption.

The Sky, the Land, the Ocean of Nature

Nature is Your nature

Nature is Your Real nature!

Being in Nature and Being in the Forest is the Best and the Most Natural Feeling Humans can Have! It is like Being in the Garden of Eden, Being in Heaven, Being at Our True Home, Being with God!

To Protect and Re-plant the Earth means to
Secure that Original Link to Ourselves, to God!

"The love for all living creatures is the most noble attribute of man."
Charles Darwin

Once You See this as The Universal Truth, You will Understand the importance of sharing Knowledge since this is the only way Society and Global Consciousness can Evolve, can Awaken!

We don't have to discuss Secrets of the Universe now, but We Must address the Environmental Future of Our Civilisation.

No matter Your beliefs or understandings about Life,
Ecology is, therefore, the One fundamental Reality
that We should Entertain with Urgency!

One change We must make is to limit the buying of industrial produce, instead choosing to buy Locally, Organic, from regional Farmers.

There is Nothing that Anyone needs to Stop doing more totally
or with more force than finding Healthier Alternatives
that do not abuse the Environment.

My hopes, goals, and ideas revolve primarily around
the Worldwide Ecological Revival. The Reestablishment
of Nature as The Main and Foremost Driving Force in Life

Forest

"I went to the woods because I wished to live deliberately, to front only the essential facts of life, and see if I could not learn what it had to teach, and not, when I came to die, discover that I had not lived." **Henry David Thoreau**

To Preserve and Re-plant the Forests is to Heal Ourselves!

An Eternal Forest. There is something private about it, a strangely personal closeness. It is the most primal of experiences when One is immersed in the mystery of their unknown origin & meaning!

This is Ultimately and Fundamentally linked to Our search for understanding the Nature of Reality in the Constant Stare of the Universe. It is this promise of discovering new landscapes, losing Your limited self, and feeling Free & Unlimited in its Raw Nature!

The Forest is a Natural time-warp trip into the Now!
A natural miracle of growth, a lush shadowy paradise,
a magical living room of abundant Life and freshness,
and an overflowing blossoming oasis of flora & fauna.
Like a labyrinth, it is a tapestry of endless possibilities.

It is a Source of endless inspiration in myths & legends.
The Source of real magic & beauty, authentic with all the
unique types of Trees. As in the mythical stories, it has all
the idyllic dream-like details of natural sites & scenes.
So it's not just Nature. It has a Soul embedded!
A timeless essence of being free in the wilderness
of not so wild but just right, tranquil forestry

*　*　*

The Earth is an Architect of Time in Space, of Matter meets an Energy

Shaman of Light

To walk with a wooden staff as a natural wanderer and consciously
recognise a beautiful phenomenon of Being is to Honour One's
Spiritual Ancestry and Abide in the Grace of God.

As I Walk this Forest, I take my Rightful Place
in this Cosmic Arena of Light as a Shaman of
the Present Moment and Voice of Natural Life.

I Bear the Animal Spirit, The Soul of Trees, and
Bless the Sacred Soil, As I Bridge Heaven & Earth,
Channelling these Energies of Sky & Ground,
Manifesting the Centrepoint to Inner Knowing,
a True Nature's Intelligence, with which We Celebrate this
Relationship of coming Together in various shapes & forms,
by Recognising the One Holy Origin, in God!

As God created Nature,
She Provides Us with Air to Breathe,
a Soil To Eat From,
the Water to Drink,
and Matter to Create from.

God Gave Us Everything through Nature.

Everything We've used, it came from Nature!

So keep Blessing and Thanking the Mother,
as We give Our Thanks to God Herself:

Thank You, Mother Earth and God,
for giving Us a Chance to Co-create this
Experience, Experiencing the Experience!

It is this Appreciation of the Circle of Life, of
Understanding this Communion with Existence at Large,
that really Makes Us Be Our True Selves,
ReWilding as Yourself!

When You look at Trees,
They don't think about the coming night or yesterday's rain.
They're only always & ever-fully dedicated to Being Themselves.

*Listen to the Whispers of those Ancient Trees, for I heard
Their Talk of Wisdom, and so They Spoke of Peace!*

Within that Wise Music in the Forest, find out
how Your Being Resonates with Nature, and
Feel this Universal Truth in its Essence.

Create Your Language,
Your Authentic Way from the Heart!
Keep Carrying and Repeating these Prayers of
Heartfelt Thankfulness. Walk with them Every Day in Joy.
Talk to the Great Divine One Life.
Whisper how Humble but Proud You are to
Receive these Treasures of Knowing the Secrets of Stars!
Serving The Higher Realm of Seen & Unseen.
Natural Life's Way!

Keep Blessing, Thanking, and Receiving the Healing Oneness,
and Give these Fruits of Nourishment back
to Your Community,
as LOVE

*   *   *

"We hear your message, to preserve, to flourish, to celebrate!"
Jesse Wolf Hardin

<u>Mother Healing</u>

We Hear You, Oh Great Mother!
We have received the warning &
locked down the entire system.
Now, it's the Time for Healing!

You can rejuvenate as We Rest.
You can filter Your Oceans,
You can clean Your Skies,
You can clean Your Soil,
You can refresh Your Lungs,
Your Forests, and Plankton.

These Energies Link Us to
the Universal scale of things
& give Us Life, Here on Earth,
as You are generous to provide
Us with the Gift of Life, for Free!

Make Our Breath be of fresh Air, &
fill Our days with exuberance again!
Teach Us to sense Our Inner knowing,
Our intuition, insight, & true intelligence.

It is this Blessing that We Honour Now,
as Our Ancestors have done for ages,
as They Sang to Your Heartbeat,
as They Moved with Your Seasons.

Now We remember Oh Great Mother,
how it is to be One & Whole again,
under Your Maternal Protection,
Your Holy Spirit, Your God, as
She gives Us the Soul to Be.

You are Our anchor again. Our
path, Our stream, Our Nature!

In this time of crisis, We will
Re-establish the Lifeblood Bond.
We will Re-awaken to Your Song,
We will See the Night Sky again.

When We Open Our Hearts, then
the mind becomes a tool. For it calls
forth these Souls of Ours to Feel as
One Life, Not Separate from You,
but Entangled & Rich in Being.

We are but Walking Trees,
Protectors of the Forests,
Wanderers on the Seas.

We Hear the Call,
We Feel the Change,
We Heal with You,

We Walk as One

*   *   *

As I Abide Here in Awareness

I Love You Unconditionally – Earth
As I Love You more than Myself – The World
I Drink from the Fountain of Life – Ocean
I Breathe in the Space in Time – Air
I Walk through the Garden of Wonder – Nature

And Release You as We Heal Together

Trees

I want You to Feel the Trees by understanding their
importance and significance for All Life on Earth!
Around 40% of the Earth's oxygen is produced by the 60,000 species
of Trees. They are an invaluable resource. Trees create Forests, home to
80% of Land animals, as well as helping the ground to retain water, they
communicate through their roots & fungi, and help prevent landslides.
Trees create soil from their decomposition. From Trees We can produce
wood, paper and medicines.

Wilderness must stay Wild! Trees are, along with Plankton,
the most important Living Organisms on Earth!

Trees have a relaxing and therapeutic effect on Our mind/body temple.
With their Natural presence, they slow down thought processes and
correspondingly reduce stress levels. Among other effects, a Tree:
*"Boosts the immune system, lowers blood pressure, improves mood,
increases ability to focus, improves creativity, accelerates recovery
from surgery or illness, increases energy level, improves sleep,
reduces allergies, increases self-esteem and mental wellbeing."*

Earthing, grounding, and walking barefoot:
*"Involves consciously connecting with one's forest surroundings by engaging
all five senses. Smelling the air and the musty scent of damp soil; listening to
the bird song and the wind in the branches; looking around you at the form
of trees, the patterns in the bark and the light streaming through the canopy;
touching the bark of trees, the damp moss and feeling the warmth of the
sun as it breaks through the leaves; and tasting the freshness in the air."*

There are three trillion Trees, but that is half of the original number.
Even if We re-plant all the lost Trees, it would still not be sufficient
enough to fight the CO2, so cutting down on fossil fuels is crucial too!
If We want any sustainable present & future for Us and Our children,
We have to ask Ourselves: How does Our lifestyle help this
transformative process

201

Language of Creation

Let's join Our hands with Existence in
this Healing frenzy entirely made of Source!

Let's lash Our egos out so that the only Language We
can communicate with is One of the long-forgotten Trees,
whose Ancient Dialect reveals itself when We Start Speaking
in Tongues. That Universal connection that keeps Us
Remembering Who We really are: Nature!

As Humans in Our Natural state, We exist primarily for
nothing else but to serve as Receivers of this Divine Cosmic
Energy. That is the Phenomenon of Being, of Life Itself, which
Heals Us & Mystifies Us, so that We have a Living Strength
of Force To keep Blessing this Earth, that Freely gives
Us this Place to Live and all the Space to Breathe.

We are the Channellers of this beautiful Engine of Creation.
We're in the Middle of the Universal LARGE & small Scale. Our
Awakened Awareness is the intermedium of Understanding,
of Appreciation, that the Blessing of Life needs for it to be
Spread & Passed Unto the Entire chain of Existence.

In this Grand Procession of Living Life, find out what
Your Heart really likes, and then all the Doors of Knowing
will Open up right before Your Glowing Eyes!

SUN always Shines the Same, Life is always LIGHT!

Align Yourself with these Universal Truths. Stay above
changing circumstances by knowing that Your Soul, Spirit,
and Inner Wisdom are always Here and that You can always
remain Conscious of this, and, thus, take Responsibility
for choosing only a Healthy, Grateful Attitude!

Nature is Magical and, by that, I mean Beautiful, Special,
Original, Natural, Authentic, Hypnotic, and Ancient.

I didn't mention Love, for there is no Love in Nature!
There is only Peace and Life as it Is.
A Tree doesn't love another Tree;
they exist at the mercy of weather and climate.
An Animal doesn't love another Animal;
they live by instincts and inherited behaviours.
The Air doesn't love Clouds;
they are a by-product of the Earth.

*Love is an attribute of the Soul, it is the quality of feeling
un-separated from Others, as We are not separate from the All.*
An inability to awaken Love within Oneself leads to separation,
intolerance, war, and destruction as manifestations of the ego.

Love is the Evolutionary pulse of Conscious Beings.
Nature doesn't need to Love, It's Created by Her.
To Be Love & Peace is Your Responsibility!
Cherish this Understanding, Feel It.
Awaken the Courage to Act and Embody
Your Highest Self Constantly!
That is the Holiest Blessing in Life,
To Acknowledge it as Sacred,
As it is Real

*   *   *

*Mother Nature is the Most
Amazing Dream Imagined by God,
Put Into Creation,
She,
Supreme Architect of Biology*

<u>Venerate</u>

My Heart Venerates Your Soul's Spirit!

*An Entire Universe of God's Mysterious Ways, Conspired with The
World's History of Events, to Culminate in One Essential Point in Space,
to Agree & Decide, that it's the Right Moment in Time,
to Create YOU, my Dear Humankind.*

For as You Know! Every Action has an Equal & Opposite Reaction.
As per the Chaos Theory: a Butterfly flapping its Wings in Africa,
sets a Climate of Motion that ends up as a Hurricane in Florida.

As You See, We are the Conundrum of Eternity's Wish,
Will, and Need, to Recognise Itself through Yourself.
That's How Important You Are!

You Exist on this Majestic Plane We call the Earth and as the Sun's
Rays touch Your every New Day, they flatter You Gently as
the Beauty of Nature You know We are a part of!

*"A human being is a part of the whole called by us universe,
a part limited in time and space. He experiences himself,
his thoughts and feeling as something separated from
the rest, a kind of optical delusion of his consciousness.
Our task must be to free ourselves from this prison by
widening our circle of compassion to embrace all living
creatures and the whole of nature in its beauty."* **Einstein**

We have come to this Unique Period in the Modern Age,
where Our Global Community counts 8 billion Friends.

That's how Generous Mother Earth Is; that's how Artistic She
wants to be even if it means sacrificing Other precious Life forms,
such as Animals, Plants, and Her very Earth Itself!

Through Continental Filtration of Waters,
and Rotting Biological Substrate of all kinds of Cells,
where the decomposition of Living Organisms Creates Soil,
the Minerals from the Universe, Mountains and Seas gather,
and as the Inner Core of Warmth spurts itself
out of Volcanos as Liquid Magma,
it is this Circulation of Life Energy,
mixed with Soul Essence, which Transcends
the Inanimate Matter, and by means of Morphogenesis
gives You Complete and Outmost Body Freedom & Power
to Envisage and Co-create, Magically, Any Idea of Self,
and so Overwhelmingly forces Us to Die,
whereby the only Duty We have
is to Live Forevermore!

So this goes for All,
as We are in this Together,
even though many are Oceans apart.

There is no difference between Us!
No difference between You & Me.

For the Spirit feels the Same,
as Our Soul bears no Name,
it lets Our ego enjoy the Fame,
thereby God took all the Blame,
presuming She found no Shame,
intending to express and Share!

With this Understanding,
Remember Always!

My Heart Venerates

Your Soul's Spirit

Symbiotic Pulse

God is so Unconditionally Loving and Infinitely
Conscious of the Universe that He abides as One with it All.

On Earth exists two Worlds: One Natural, another Human.
You, as Consciousness, are aware of both. You Transfix them!
Nature is a fully integrated and civilised society, while the Human's
is developing, uncivilised mess. I like the Natural World more, for
it is Original with no nonsense in its pristine & supreme form.

Nature is God and Humans are still learning to be natural,
trying to survive its madness and be in harmony with Nature.

And She changes Our mood, She is Our True Home, but people forget
that. That's why it is essential to go to the park daily and experience
wild Nature weekly. Or better yet, to live in Nature altogether.

Mother Nature is Our Goddess! We live on and from Her.
We breathe Her; We eat Her; We use Her for everything We build.
She is Innocent and, We could say, Unconditionally Loving, as She's lying
naked all around Us, free & open, susceptible to Our greed or mercy.
We can abuse Her, or We can use Her the right way, as We learn
to Feel and therefore Know to be the Conscious part of Her.

We are the Conscious extension of Nature !

Every gift & gesture of Love is unconditional, so imagine how
much of such Love We should feel towards Nature, Earth, and
the Universe, All of which exist as the Gift for Our Conscious Life.

The fact that We exist in this existence where existence exists freely,
and We exist freely in it, implies We feel unconditional love towards
existence. Even more so, We know through meditation that We
are One with existence and separation is an optical illusion.

Nature is an immovable force.
Self-replicated, Self-organising, and Self-governing,
it is an ever-evolving entity; it exists of its own accord.
It is literally another World with a personal & private Life,
but it doesn't think, and it doesn't have an opinion.
It doesn't hold grudges and it doesn't fight. It interacts and
it doesn't kill. It consumes Itself for the benefit of Itself.
It can be destroyed, and She will bounce back.
It can be cut down and She will grow up.
It can be killed, and She will come alive.
It can be obliterated on one planet
and She will re-emerge on another.

It is always there, whether anyone acknowledges it or not.
It will Live forever, with or without You!

Nature Lives as Nature Breathes. Humans depend on Nature 100%.
Nature doesn't need Humans. Humans need Nature!

*Nature is an Ultimate & Primal Religion. It doesn't have to be written
down; it doesn't need to be taught; it already Exists perfectly on its Own!
She is Our Life on Earth and is the Highest Teacher of Humanity.*

This Nature's Intelligence, or as **Rupert Sheldrake** calls it,
Morphic Resonance, is a type of collective remembrance.

All You have to do is be Still,
Feel Her Symbiotic Pulse and Listen
to Her Unwavering Support.

Nature is in the Universe.
The Universe is the Nature of it All.

Nature Is as **CONSCIOUSNESS** IS,
tHere is no separation Here!
It is All ONE in GOD, and so are YOU

CHAPTER 9

CONSCIOUSNESS

Consciousness

Consciousness Is.
Consciousness simply Is.
Consciousness is simply the Knowing.
Consciousness is the Knowing of Being.
Consciousness is the Knowing of Being Aware.

It is the knowing of presence, the constant of perceiving.
It's the knowing by which all Our experience is known.
It is the one undeniable fact of knowing the experience.
The basic existential fundament – a journeyless destination.

You can think about it, but in that way, it will escape You by the rule of fleeting thoughts. So to know Consciousness, You must Know it by Experiencing it. You do this by stopping all resistance, all the efforts, and by Being Still. From this Knowing, We know We cannot grasp it by any attempts. We know it can only be Itself. It is where We relax the efforts and Be as it Is.

Consciousness doesn't start, nor does it end. It also can't be named, termed, or titled. It is the background upon which Your entire Life is playing out. It is Your Life. It is Life. The Life of Beings, as Beingness.

Writing about Consciousness is literally like writing about Air. There is no personality involved in it, yet the person is experiencing, reflecting, realising, and writing about the absence of the very person that can not be touched, approached, seen, heard, comprehended, for Consciousness is not the object of knowledge, but the subjectness of Beingness. Here, there is no tending towards or going outwards, and We don't access it; We lose Ourselves by allowing IT to Be, dropping all & every concept of the self, remaining selfless in the full emptyless abidance.

In Consciousness, Our Being streams Itself into Existence,
flowering as a blossoming Lotus from the mud of matter and
unconsciousness, penetrating dimensionless illusions
and sense perceptions of the *Phantom Self.*

Ramana has given Us profound insights into such freedom:

"Who am I?

The gross body which is composed of the seven humours (dhatus), I am not;
the five cognitive sense organs, viz. the senses of hearing, touch, sight,
taste, and smell, which apprehend their respective objects,
viz. sound, touch, colour, taste, and odour, I am not;
the five cognitive senseorgans, viz. the organs of speech, locomotion,
grasping, excretion, and procreation, which have as their respective functions
speaking, moving, grasping, excreting, and enjoying, I am not;
the five vital airs, prana, etc., which perform respectively
the five functions of in-breathing, etc., I am not;
even the mind which thinks, I am not;
the nescience too, which is endowed only with the residual impressions
of objects, and in which there are no objects and no functioning's,
I am not.

If I am none of these, then who am I?

After negating all of the above-mentioned as 'not this', 'not this',
that Awareness which alone remains - that I am."

One can't go behind Awareness. It can not be cut, shared, separated,
divided. From this, We know there Is only One Awareness, the One
Consciousness within which Universal Existence has appeared.

So it can't be measured, captured, calculated, observed,
and it can't even be known, for it is the Knowing Itself.

It is Your essential
irreducible Nature,
as the Awareness

Consciousness

Being Aware – the Awareness Itself!

Consciousness, the only thing You've ever and You'll ever Be,
but the one essential thing You've never been Conscious of.

For most people, this natural 'state' is always covered by thoughts,
and identifying with those thoughts creates an ego or illusory sense of
self. All this is happening privately in Your mind, and when You add
power to thoughts, there they arise, Emotions as Feelings!

But You don't feel Consciousness – You Are It!
You are One with perceiving Reality.

The point on Your body where You sense it the
most is an area in the middle of the forehead
– the Third Eye.

When was the last time You were aware of Your breathing?
This is Your primary entry point for Being Aware.
Once You drop all the physical & mental effort,
You are Aware of Being Aware!

Everything happening in The World, the Universe,
is playing on the Screen of Consciousness,
where Your Life is a movie that You believe to be real.

To indulge in ignorance is to be lost in the World: illusion.
To carry the weight of the World is an act of total compassion; illumination.
To transcend it is the greatest achievement; liberation.

Unconsciousness implies seeking happiness outside
of Yourself, while Consciousness is Peace.
"The Peace which Surpasses All Understanding."

Consciousness doesn't care about good or bad, about the creation & destruction of the Universe, the forming of galaxies & planets, the emergence of biological life, the killing & reproduction of animals, or the birth & death of humans. It has no knowledge of polarity, no investment in the future, and no obligation towards the past. It can never do anything outside of the Now!

Consciousness has Nothing to do with Spirituality, Religion, Faith, Belief, Magic, Cults, Science, New Age, Old Age, Dogma, Superstition, Karma, Thinking, Philosophy, Humans, or God. But these have Everything to do with Consciousness! All of these arise within Consciousness. All are existential phenomena within It. All of those appear in Consciousness, which is the One & Only Constant – the Beingness.

Consciousness Is Your Essential Irreducible Nature!
You are a Self-individualised clinging bundle of thoughts. You are made of Consciousness that is projecting Itself as an experiential, localised, personalised piece of paraphernalia.

In this way, Consciousness knows itself as Itself, through an agency of the mind, as a veiling within Itself. Since there is no separation between Consciousness & Consciousness, Consciousness then does nothing. The mind does everything, until the appearance of separation seems to recognise itself within its illusory reality.

There is no more truth to this reality as these bolts of thoughts than truth to the characters created in Your dream. There Is Only Consciousness!

"Consciousness is that in which all experience appears, it is that with which all experience is known, and it is that out of which all experience is made." **Rupert Spira**

In Alive Beings, It Abides as *Wakeful Alertness, Present Aliveness, Focus, Awareness, Pure Presence, Attention, Aware Looking, Stillness, and The Knowing!*

Eventually, We all need to find this as Our Own Truth.
Which, if properly investigated & observed, is the same
and only enduring Fact that We are Conscious,
no matter the outside experience.

Whether You are an animal, plant, stone, Human, Alien,
or Galaxy, experience is always through Consciousness.

It is the identification with the outer form that
creates the sense of separation, the feeling of I, Me, and Mine.
But, upon closer examination, this delusion falls quickly when
exposed to the Light of One's True Self – Consciousness.

You can spend a Lifetime being unaware of these facts,
and it would have been the World that was pulled
over Your eyes, distracting You from the Truth.

The Truth You've been avoiding for so long, by ignoring
Your Natural Inner Guidance, Intuition, Consciousness,
and by blindly following the path of Worldly Illusions.

All Religions talk about this state in their own unique way,
promising Liberation in it, and thus Eternal Peace & Happiness.
All Wisdom and the Greatest philosophical secrets teach this.

And they are all True, All of It Is!
All is True once We Illuminate it
with The Light of CONSCIOUSNESS

*   *   *

Make every moment a relationship with Your open Heart,
and living that Love abides in the Light of God.

Filter Yourself Down To The Bare Light

215

Nothing

Everybody wants to be Something.
There is only One Thing I wanted to be.
I wanted to be NoThing!

And by that, I mean Consciousness.

The only thing You already Are, and will ever Be.
The most effortless career One can ever have.

Yet, Your mind is just distracting You from
Experiencing Being Pure Consciousness.

Consciousness is *"the Superposition of Possibilities,"*
which is the Quantum Principle of its General State.

It is the Primal state of all Beings, and on top
of that, One can manifest Anything & Everything.

And You'll choose to manifest, to entertain all types of Worldly
experiences because Our bodies & minds programme themselves
naturally and artificially to seek those sensations We lack.

The primary examples being: food, drink, sleep, safety, social
comfort, procreation, satisfaction, fun, knowledge, intellect,
responsibility, power, influence, and meaning.

That is a domain of the mind's wants and needs. But
as soon as You step outsides of this never-ending
circle of perpetual Self-indulgence,

Life in its Foremost state

Begins to Shine

Thoughts

You, don't have Thoughts. Thoughts have You!
Consciousness is aware of both. In fact, You're just another Thought,
and Consciousness is Beingness prior to any appearances.

Thought can not know thought. Knowing knows thought.
The same as wood can not burn wood; fire burns wood.
A thought is like a piece of wood, a piece of solid matter in the
form of a mental type of energy. It is the activity in Consciousness.
Aligning Yourself with Consciousness Fundamentally is to awaken
One's True nature based on objective truth rather than subjective opinion.
It's reducing Oneself to the primary state – Being – observance absent
of the Self. That, however, does not mean losing the rich inner
experience, as the mind sees it, but expending such Awareness
to its fullest capacity, contrary to the mind's narrowing,
since Thoughts imply contraction of Consciousness.

"Thinking is only a small aspect of consciousness. Thought
cannot exist without consciousness, but consciousness does not
need thought. Observe your thoughts, don't believe them." **Eckhart Tolle**

From such an open space comes what mystics refer to as the Knowing
– as opposed to thinking. And it is this Freedom where creativity, art,
intuition, insights, wisdom, Love, understanding & Knowing all arise.

To allow this state, We return to Conscious breathing, an Inner peace,
staying as Awareness, observing reality as it is, seeing things as
they are, and in that non-attachment, experiencing the Timeless
sense of being, the ground of all perception: God, Zen, Tao.
Stay Rooted in Being, Become Aware of Breathing. Focus Attention
on that Presence. It's the only Lasting Experience there Is.
Upon close examination of the Self, One finds only That which is Aware.
When that recognition makes the full circle, The Pure Beingness remains.
That is the Fundamental Nature of Self-Awareness

Awareness of Self

The only certainty in Existence One can be assured of
is His own Awareness. Even His identity is a thought, a sense of
separation/individuality. As We have explored throughout this book,
all the separation is illusory and temporary; it is a brief appearance
in Consciousness. As One starts to recognise this inevitable passing
of all illusions, He will be orienting His focus on remaining Aware.
He will be the witnessing Awareness. This, He knows intuitively
and Self-consciously. Awareness is Our prime state!

"I'm addicted to Awareness" **Dreaming-Bear Baraka Kanaan**

Even to say that Consciousness is aware is incorrect. Instead, the
Awareness of Self is aware of Itself. And Consciousness simply IS.

With that recognition, the whole sense of Self dissolves.
Consciousness doesn't have to be or do anything to be more of what
It already Is. It is always Constant, Uninterrupted, and Unchanging!

Therefore, no outside action or change can move it. No external influence
or force can sway it away! With enough Presence, no internal conflict
matters either, for they fade away naturally as this inner dimension opens.

You have never had or experienced anything outside of Consciousness,
yet You remain unaware of It. By shifting the focus from the Out/In,
thus recognising the shaky character of thoughts, choose to remain
firmly focused Out, without the need to go Back\In! When You sit
& drop Your ego, You start channelling wisdom and intuitive insights.

Who You think You are is a collection of thoughts You keep repeating to Yourself.
What You really are is the Looking Itself, no past or future, which are memories.

You are Aware Presence, new in each moment, You are
Beingness having the experience of Knowing.

You are not the perceiver or perceived, You are Perceiving Itself.
You are not *a voice in Your head that is just saying things,*
You are the Awareness of it, which is Aliveness, Openness.

It is only to the degree of belief in a separate self that determines
unpleasantness of experiencing. The only reason one enjoys is ego.
The only reason one suffers is ego. The middle ground is peace, is
contentment – the very sacred presence of Awareness.

Observe Yourself and The World without judgment,
Invite Thyself to be Known through Awareness,
Allow The Witness to be Present in The Ever Now!

Even romantic and unconditional Love will fade away as body & soul
dissolve back to the Light of Eternal Darkness, but underlying Being will linger,
and will Be. Let Our Presence speak of Our Love, even when We fall silent.

The only thing there is to Life, Is Awakening, but it is in Our
conditioned Human nature to delay it as long as possible,
to have a richer experience of subtle ways of reality.

Nothing else ever truly matters than this State of Being Present:
to Know Thyself as Awareness, to be the Knower of Experience,
and to Abide in this Space where Experience is Known.

You were born with only Consciousness, and everything else was added
later. But on Your deathbed, You will remember that it was all added.

Then, Pure Consciousness will Remain

*   *   *

Study at the University of following Your own Heart and Intuition!
It will lead You to the exact space & time You want to be,
resulting in an Awareness of each & every moment of experience

Pure Consciousness

Pure Consciousness is What We Are!
Everything else is Our Imagination.

From that point of Infinite Awareness, Everything exists in
the state of Potential & Possibilities. You judge nothing by the level
of its condition. You See & Recognise everything by its Potential.

*A leaf that falls from a tree is the same as the one still on
that tree. Rich people are the same as poor people;
educate poor people, and They could be rich.*

History can go many ways and reach numerous destinies,
but We observe only one of those at any given time. It
is important to be aware of many other possibilities
which a Life can play out without becoming
attached to the actual witnessed outcome.

*All Things Change, Nothing Stays Same.
It's the Impermanence of All Things!*

The Universe didn't always exist, and
now it does, until it goes back to sleep.
The One Fundamental Construct We can
find is Within, as Pure Consciousness

*   *   *

*Before You Learn – Do, Before You Taste – Touch,
Before You Feel – Think, Before You See – Observe,
Before You Know – Reason, Before You Are – just Be,
Before I Am – IT IS*

Spaciousness

Look right in front of You into empty Space!
There is nothing obvious there; it's empty.
That is Consciousness, Stillness, Emptiness, Beingness!

Now imagine if We're to create a Person there, give Them a mind
& story, and They Come to Life, subsequently believing what They
perceive as body, mind, thoughts, and That Sense of I, Me, and Mine.
All those experiences are happening in the Empty Space that was
empty just a moment before, and it still is; it gives a platform
upon which the Story of Our lives is playing out.

And it is playing as unconsciousness. As We know, Those
individuals who do become profoundly aware of this Space,
of Their true essence, and thus align Themselves as that
everlasting peace eventually don't have anything left to play.
We're Consciousness experiencing the mind and no-mind
of the Universe, of God, creating different points in Space!

Everyone's perspective is equally valid and significant. From
Consciousness' point of view, a homeless man has the same importance
as the President of the Country, for Consciousness doesn't make a
difference. It simply observes as a camera, without thoughts or
opinions. It doesn't separate or divide, it looks at things as they are.
All connected and One within that Ever-present, Everlasting Space.

You are that emptiness out of which Your mind produces such
variety of shapes & forms, this richness We call Life: Love.

From dust You are born, from emptiness You are conceived,
into dust You will return, and into Spaciousness You will recede.

Who Are You? You Are That!
Be That Now

221

Black Colour

The Most Common Sight in the Universe is the Pitch Black;
It is Complete Darkness – a Total Absence of Light.
Ether, Emptiness, and Nothingness.

It is like Pure Consciousness – The One
Fundament that gives Rise to all Possibilities of Existence.

What Colour is the Medium in which the Universe,
Darkness, and Light exist then? Such must
be the True Colour of Consciousness.
It is the Colour of Pure Beingness.
This Colour is made of all other colours
prior to them being Born via the Light.

You are trying to fill the Void with colours,
which is impossible! For it is unreal, illusory,
and made of thoughts. It is Self-created and will
dissolve only in the Attentive recognition of One's True Being.

Attention is then the ability to be fully aware and own Yourself in
the Present moment. The ability to Control Yourself Completely.

Your Own Peace, Your Own Consciousness is the Power
and the Entry to this Senseless Perception. You don't
have to do anything to be in such Aware Peace;
Just to Be is enough for Beingness in Bliss!

There is Freedom in Peace, Freedom from identification.
Freedom in Observing without judgment.
Freedom in Not wanting anything from anyone.

So Happiness comes from outside things,
but Joy from an Inner state of Peace

The Secret

CONSCIOUSNESS !

That Magic Spicy Word, Echoing Your Greatness!

It is the only Cosmological Constant.
It is the Ultimate Mantra!

Whereby, repeating it an infinitesimal number of times,
in just a Single moment of Entirety of Forevers Infinity, You are
Performing a Surgically Precise Operation on the thoughts in Your
mind, thus Liberating You from the false, self-inflicted tendencies of
seeing everything in Existence as separate and distant, since it's
far away from You. This makes You run around the World,
searching for happiness, but upon finding only betrayal,
rejection, & lies, You're left exhausted, broken, & alone,
in the privacy of Your own habitual Self-talk:

Why do I trouble an already troubled mind?
How can I unsee what I have seen,
all the pain and all the sorrow?

This then forces You to Reorganise the game.
It Pushes You to Rearrange Your Life. So You sit in Stillness,
observing the reoccurring passing Worlds inside Your Inner World.
Noticing how whatever appears, You're always an ever-present
Witness as the Awareness. By Experiencing and Realising this
Liberating state of Pure Beingness, You are Illuminated by the
Light of Consciousness, and therefore Are Lifted from Your ego,
which in turn Gives You the Complete Freedom to Recreate
within this Newfound Glory – to Transform Yourself
into The Self You have always Known and
have Forever wanted to Be!

This Expended Awareness then
Opens Up Your Doorways of Perception, Your
Intuitive Knowing, Your Innate Intelligence, and All the
Capacities of Understanding are Now at Your disposal.

By using this Inner-found Cosmic Code of Wisdom, You
Reverberate throughout Space and all Dimensions of Time
as if Sucked into the Blackhole and Blown out of the
Wormhole of a Multiversal projected Hologram,
where this Space Travel Odyssey Began & Ends, Inside
the Rebirth of Your Forever-exploding Supernova Heart.

*That Heart is Awareness and is not a state. It's the ever-present
quality of observing all the passing states of mind as a temporary
localisation in Consciousness. When You sleep or die, there is no
mind left; there are no thoughts that would create the sense of time
& space, therefore neither would there be the feeling of I. That's the
Pure Consciousness – the absence of thoughts. And You will not
remember this, since there's nothing to remember. That's how it
feels to be dead or to sleep without dreaming. It's Nothing.
No thoughts, but Consciousness, which is always tHere,
unrecognised by anything. It just Is!*

This, then, is The Secret of The World
and The Universal Secrets:

*Infinity is the Eternal Existence of Thy Universe,
and God is One Knowledge Thereof,
as Infinite Consciousness,
as YOU*

*   *   *

*It is through Our Eyes that
the Universe is Conscious of Itself*

Expended Awareness

How much Knowledge and Understanding
is it possible to have within Our Awareness?

Base one is the Awareness of Our immediate perception through
the 5 senses, thoughts, and feelings. Then, We can extend this through
technology, such as watching TV, reading newspapers, talking on the
phone, or interacting through the internet. Finally, We can use Our
imagination to visualise existence outside of the reach of the base
senses by allowing recognition of actual & possible happenings,
such as imagining Star Civilisations.

We can thus use Consciousness to project Our
Awareness into the endless possibilities of events.

The simple practice of Understanding the World is to track any product,
Living Being, or anything back to its source. Consider this book You're
holding in Your hands. You bought it in a store, where the bookstore
employee put it on a shelf. It came yesterday by truck delivery, from
the local distribution centre, and a week ago it was shipped from a
printing warehouse in another country.

They took all the supplies from factories that produce paper & ink,
and They, in turn, sourced those materials from logging companies
and chemical factories. And all these elements come from Nature.

Try this reduction process for anything that
exists in the World, in the Universe.

Now, imagine & acknowledge an entire Global phenomenon of Life
by starting from Your base senses. Wherever You may be, become
aware of breathing, bodily sensations, thoughts, and feelings.
Look around the room, street, or Nature, be it wherever You are.

Then, Use Your imagination to See through the walls in Your mind's eye.

Know there is a family member in another room, there is a car
behind the building, or that there are hikers behind the mountain.
Use Your knowledge of the World to create The World.
Start expanding this circle of visualisation to keep projecting
possible reality. Reconstruct the World inside Your
imagination, and become fully aware of it.

That means becoming aware of a billion people driving cars right now,
or of a billion people sleeping, and a billion people working or just being
at home. And a billion people on the streets of cities & villages. The billion
people in poverty. Imagine all the people at events, in schools, hospitals,
stadiums, restaurants, ships, airplanes, and all the people in Nature.

Now, try to imagine all the Nature, animals, on all 7 Continents with
forests, meadows, deserts, lakes, and rivers. And in an entire Ocean that
occupies 99% of Living space on Earth, with some 65% of all the Life.

Go even deeper into details and realise all the trillion
molecules and countless atoms that make up the World.
The subatomic world is a final Conscious expansion.

But now direct Your Awareness in the other direction, towards the
Universe; zoom Yourself from fundamental particles, atoms, through
molecules, cells, and bodies. Fly out of the Earth to see it clearly in
front of the expended blackness of the Universe. Pass through Our
Solar system, near the Stars, and leave the Galaxy disk to see it
swirling in its total, majestic size & shape.
Move farther to observe an intergalactic space, a local Galaxy cluster, and
then an entire observable Universe. But go even more into imagination
and extend the view by going above Our Universe, to the theoretical
multiverse, infinity, and beyond. Play with Your imagination and
create an infinite number of Planets, Civilisations, and Beings.

This expansion practice is a powerful tool with which to use Our
mind, to extend Our Awareness to every corner of Existence,
to exercise how it feels to be One & All

Butterfly Effect

Consciousness is Consciousness In Continuation!

There are No moments, only the Constant of NOW.

It doesn't Act, or React. It always just IS,
and it is Universal, All-encompassing. It is the
Only Point tHere Is. The Nexus for Space & Time.

Philosophical depth is thus essential because it is in the
arena of original Human thought and the comprehension
of Existentiality that Our intellectual capacity for
Understanding Consciousness can deepen and evolve.

Consciousness then, of course, doesn't have shape or form,
but it gives a chance for these to appear, manifest, and exist.

It is not, nor does it have, thoughts. Thoughts arise as the mind,
with ego being a thought believing & drawing the sense of
identification from that feeling of I, that feeling of me & mine.

All Beings are Subject to Consciousness and No Being is
Fully Conscious, for Consciousness is Beingness Itself.

That even includes Spiritual Entities such as the Soul.
All the facets of existing Beings appear in Consciousness.

The Only True Measure of Consciousness is Freedom from
thought. To be Free as a Bird, Rock, Tree, or Unmanifested.
The mind just distracts You constantly from Realising Your
True nature, as the Ever-present State of Beingness – Isness.

Free Choice or Free Will is correspondent with Consciousness.
The more Self-awareness We have, the more Choice there is available.

Still, even that can't be tied down perfectly to make a definitive
law about it, since every present action is a by-product
of all previous experiences, causes, and effects.

*"How can we be 'free' as conscious agents if everything
that we consciously intend is caused by events in our brain that
we do not intend and of which are entirely unaware?"* **Sam Harris**

From that standpoint, even Your choice to sit in meditation for hours
results from all that has been happening in Your Life. For it gave You
the sufficient ability to control Yourself for hours, so much so that
You sit in peace completely unmoved and untroubled by thoughts.

But, for the sake of better Understanding and making a justified
correlation between Consciousness and Free Will, We can Feel
Free to make a statement that **Consciousness = Choice**!

Consciousness Implies The Ability to Control Yourself Fully.

Given the complexity of Our Civilisation, Science is the
only tool that can save Us by securing the continuation
of Life on Earth. It's only about the Way We Use It:
Unconsciously, or Intelligently & Consciously.

Therefore, this is The Paradox, since Consciousness
doesn't have External Interests; It Already Is Itself fully.
So We truly are at the Mercy of the Strangest
Universal Uncertainty Principle:
The Butterfly Effect

*   *   *

*In the Eternity of Infinite Universes,
Given Enough Time, However Improbable,
Impossible Things Will Eventually Happen*

M<u>edium</u>

For any experience to occur, there must be a Medium in
which that experience happens, and that Medium is Consciousness.

No matter what the experience is, whether it is through the mind,
body, thoughts, or even if You are left with Spirit & Soul,
ALL experience happens in Consciousness!

Therefore: *All experiences will cease to happen!*
All the thoughts, feelings, sensations, and perceptions will stop,
and only Consciousness will remain.

To put it more bluntly, all fun, pleasure, and happiness will end,
especially on Your deathbed, and once You truly experience
the dissolution of all forms, will You know Consciousness.

Ask Yourself, what is left if You don't experience the 5 senses,
if You're Aware, but can't See, Hear, Taste, Touch, and Smell?
What is left is the Only Thing that is Ever-present,
Pure Consciousness!

You can experience this Now by isolating Yourself in a
closed space, without light or sound, and remaining still.
There, is only Consciousness.

It is Always & Already Here, Right Now. It is just covered up
by the 5 senses, but mostly by mind chatter, misidentification,
and constant unconscious involvement in the action.

Consciousness is the only thing that We and Everything
else in Existence have in common.
All Our differences are diversity by which experience happens.
And once You strip Yourself naked of All the forms & states,
Consciousness is revealed.

229

In Truth, Consciousness is No thing. It is so Nothing that
it doesn't even exist. It is not even Self-awareness, but it
is the Beingness left After the ego's dissolution,
of Seeing Reality As It Is.

Like wind or a feeling, it is a Space in
which experience and Awareness of it happens.

We're always In the same amount of Consciousness,
We are just not constantly aware of it, if ever. And We
have built a World whose only function is to keep Our
minds entertained by supporting its economy, which is
the only way it can sustain itself, by being unconscious.

That artificial structure, that Status Quo, is The Matrix! The
programme of stereotypical narratives and societal norms to which We
are all enslaved. The illusion runs so deep that it makes You who You
think You are, and You're even ready to defend it with Your Life.

This Delusion of Separation, a mindful madness, is the
Original Sin, but it's the process which every Civilisation
needs to go through in its Developing Evolution.

And if it doesn't destroy itself by the internal conflicts of
its collective unconsciousness, it can survive by tackling
these problems with technological advancements.

It can build a Space Empire and survive among Stars. Outside of
any Universal dangers. It can dodge all the physical dissolution and
even live Forever, jumping from one dying Universe to another. It can
sustain itself indefinitely & forever in an infinity of shapes & forms.
But it will never for one moment leave the only Space in which
all the experiences, however lasting they may be, happen.
It will Never leave
the Now Realm,
of Consciousness

Beyond I AM

Consciousness or Awareness doesn't need any identification to justify its existence. Only the mind-made self holds on to the idea, feeling, belief, experience, or perception of I Am.

I Am is a phrase, a thought, a statement that aims to describe that individual, personal, or private experience of Itself.

But Consciousness is no mind or person, so it doesn't make any statements. Consciousness simply Is!

All statements and language come from a separate sense of self, which is the illusory sense, for it's made of thoughts that are brief appearances within Awareness. They are like a passing wind, non-existent as opposed to what continuous constant Is, which is limited experience in Consciousness. Consciousness is an Empty Air, a hollow container, and there is nothing to it other than Pure Beingness.

Since Consciousness is the natural state of all Existence, everything that We temporarily experience, no matter for how many intervals, will eventually fade away when it is not covered up by thoughts.

Consciousness is always here and once You stop resisting what Is, You are allowing more Space, more Time between thoughts, and more Awareness to shine as it naturally does.

To be more Conscious doesn't require new knowledge. It requires removing One's ignorance of Its True nature.

That is a matter of personal experience. Although outside circumstances can trigger Awakening from the mind, it is Your Own recognition of Inner Being that finally breaks the spell of thoughts.

All that We go through, all that We experience, is an
activity of the mind. When Awakening occurs, it
is a Realisation that We are Not the mind and
that We don't need to do anything in order
to be Ourselves as Pure Consciousness.

The mind is the movie, and Consciousness
is the screen upon which the movie is playing out.

What does the mind need to do to dissolve in Consciousness?

The mind needs a realisation of itself, which comes from being Still,
by noticing the inevitable passing of all experiences. It needs to
stop playing, stop acting, stop engaging, and dramatising.
Stop taking the movie so seriously & personally, and
recognise that it is aware within Consciousness.

Consciousness is always fully and only Itself.
Consciousness never ever does anything.

It is Our mind which seeks & searches for the answers.
It prays, meditates, comprehends, and eventually dissolves
within its True nature, in Abiding as Awareness, in Stopping
the Resistance. In such recognition, such comprehension and
understanding, the mind relaxes In & back on itself. It finds
the answer to all questions in just Being Still, thus,
letting the Awareness be as it naturally Is.

That is the Freedom from Yourself,
the Letting Go of Attachment,
and the Relaxing of the Senses.

Here, even to have the thought *I Am* is too much.
Even to blink is too much, for Consciousness is too busy being
only Conscious, being only continuously Aware, without the will,
need, or desire to involve Itself in perceptual experience.

The fundamental technique to abide as Consciousness is Self-enquiry.
We keep asking Ourselves *To whom has this thought arisen*, answering it with
To me. Then upon asking *Who Am I*, the mind will come to a standstill.
One should keep asking these questions as long as the mind subsides
completely in Awareness as the only possible eternal answer.

Rupert Spira has the best way of bringing Our Awareness
back to Consciousness by simply asking: *AM I AWARE?*

Now, what does all of this mean, and
how does it relate to Our day-to-day Life?

The more Conscious You are, the more Life You will Abide In.
The more in mind You are, the more of Life will You Miss Out on.

Once We Align Ourselves with this Universal and Personal Truth,
there are no limits to achieving Inner Peace. Then the real Joy of Being
is to share that Bliss and make Other People Happy by Reminding
Them to Awaken the same Power Within Themselves.

Unconditional Love and Appreciation for this Blessing of Being is
Our True nature, and the mind is a tool through which We express
Our gratitude in the Art of giving Respect and Love To All.

When We Understand the Power of the Law of Attraction and
how every intention, thought, and feeling affects the wider
World, We can naturally choose to Send Only Love Out.
That is Spirituality, Consciousness, Soul!

This stands as the Fundamental Nature of Reality, of the
Nature of Consciousness, and the way experience is created
by losing Ourselves in *The WORLD*, in the mind's play,
which leads us to missing on the Very Nature in
which the movie is playing out,
Consciousness Itself

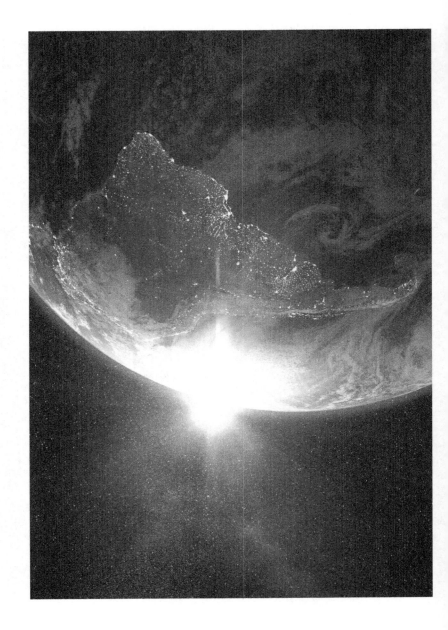

CHAPTER 10

THE WORLD

The Earth

The Earth is a Closed System!

It is an interplay of Universal Forces and Global differences
of Hot/Cold Energies of Matter. For this reason, there is Pressure
that creates Weather Patterns, Ocean Streams, and Currents.
The wind is a side effect of that pressure in Climate.

Forests & Vegetation are the Lungs while Algal PLANKTON, Kelp,
and Prochlorococcus Phytoplankton are The Oxygen Factory of Earth!
They are Floating Biological Continents.

An open ocean makes You appreciate the uniqueness of Conscious
Human life on the land. If a Self-reflective Consciousness is unable
to develop in water, it is only obvious that it took evolution to
reach the zenith of Self-awareness as a Human life form.

"The Earth is a miracle. Life remains a mystery." HOME

Humanity has added 5 billion Souls over the past 100 years,
putting more pressure on The Delicate Balance of Nature. It is not
a question of If, but When the Entire Ecosystem will collapse!

*"The pollution of the planet is only an outward reflection of an inner
psychic pollution: millions of unconscious individuals not taking
responsibility for their inner space."* Eckhart Tolle

Every Year We Live Is Now More Crucial
than All the Previous Years Combined!

Can We make it through the Challenges Ahead,
Transforming This Society Into one that is Green-based?

Or will We just have as much fun as We can, while We can

237

System

"No problem can be solved from the same level of consciousness that created it."
Einstein

The System creates people! Depending on Your place of birth, You're likely the mirror of it. By diving deep into the nature of the Self, One can align Himself with His True nature. That nature is Consciousness! It's the same anywhere in The World and identical anywhere in the Universe. The System is built on complete ignorance towards Our nature and Our true Human needs. It forces Us to live this way simply by being born into the System, but if You think You enjoy this, that You have freedom & fun, You're ignorant of the entire and higher consequential symbiosis of Life on Earth. We have no more time to live in this ignorance, which is forced on Us by this unconscious entity We call the System, which is Our collective unconscious, feeding itself in circles of denial.

We feel free within the System because that's what the System is built to do – to give Us the feeling of freedom. But this is illusory, temporary security. The reality of its fragility will quickly become obvious if the System collapses. Without it, We have to figure out Life for Ourselves; shelter, food, safety. Suddenly the reality of Nature becomes obvious – how it's the only real permanent structure, the real authority, temporally obscured by the unconscious System, just as the ego obscures Our Awareness. We live in an incredibly fragmented World and We have a responsibility to take Our Awareness back from the System, and return to Our True Selves. Since Existence doesn't have built-in meaning, We give meaning to Life. With meaning, We get the intention, which is the basis of Will. And the base of Our Life is the monetary system, which basically exists for profit. The Governments don't run the Countries alone. Corporate interests with their lobbyists, do too. We don't employ people and scientists to find the best, most economical, healthiest, most efficient way to live; We employ Them to figure out how to make the most profit. That is a Fundamental Error of Human Civilisation! As money has become the driving force of Life, People's Will has been hijacked by an unconscious System.

Their indoctrinated mind overshadows Their Consciousness, and in the absence of reason, We have built the World as if We believe We'll have natural resources forever. To justify the current mess, there must be corporate & private interests. We are slaves even though Everybody wants Freedom.

"Until you change the way money works, you change nothing." **Michael Ruppert**

Food growth is already using every usable area, including hills, lakes, and Sea. Half of The World's forests are lost! We have polluted air, water, and soil. Half the people on Earth don't even have a car or basic energy necessities, while the bomb is already exploding as the Ecosystem is Collapsing! We should have preserved more than Half of The World's Wilderness. But for the last 250 years, We have kept striving for economic growth as Our medical, industrial, and agricultural revolutions allowed for plunder to excess.

Overpopulation is not a myth! We have 5 billion extra people living on the Future Nature & Generations Credit. But Life is a Truly Remarkable Phenomenon. Everything We have & know now is thanks to the Entire History of Progress. It's Time to Use this Knowledge and Focus on Transforming Ourselves so that We can Live in Sustainable Health.

This happens by sharing the knowledge of how to go deeper into the Self, which is through Spiritual practice and Meditation, Nature, Intellectual study, and Heart Unconditional Love! Those Individuals can influence the way the System is working, giving Birth to a New Generation of People who will benefit from such a better System from the Start.

The problems in the World are side-effects of the System. The System exists for the System to exist; it doesn't exist to deal with the World's problems. Trying to fix the World's problems within the System is just another side-effect of it. The change that We want to see in the World is not happening because We are still the same.

"Be the Change You want to See in the World!" **Mahatma Gandhi**

To change the System, the System needs to Change!

We Can Change It

Civilisation

I'm talking to You as another fellow Human Being, the walking &
waking intelligence on this Planet. Just look around You, the Earth is
overrun by Us – overly built up, cemented, and ploughed. And for what?
Because We can't get real and re-examine Our priorities. We can't
overcome Our basic needs, call them reptilian, animalistic,
mammalistic, or Nietzsche's *"Human, all too human."*

Civilisation usually implies: all citizens are protected under the rule
of law and are free within the given sets of conduct. Cities with relevant
institutions and roads are built, armed security is installed, a wider range
of possibilities to progress within the range of knowledge. All in all,
it means the faster evolution of Humanity, and the type of
evolution is that going to be is determined by the will of people.

The essential Human nature is happiness. Humans come from other
Humans, so it is obvious, We are the so-called 'social animals,' to quote
Aristotle. We're centred around communities, but the modern world is
fast breaking that base by isolating Us into smaller & smaller families.

We're left with basically no relatives and often living a solitary life,
with no partner or children. We have become preoccupied with careers
and individuality to the point of the unsustainability of community,
so the modern world runs on cheap and foreign labour to
keep the economy going and keep the western lifestyle possible.

We've known of such a situation in almost every Civilisation in history.
It is the same story of development. Civilisation, an Empire, or a Country
becomes so out of touch with reality living on the high standard that
They lose the basic Human qualities that made Them great and
prosperous in the first place, until there are no original People left to
sustain the continuation of such a structure. That circular karma of
Civilisation is embedded into the very ideology of striving for a
leisure lifestyle where the community becomes gradually ignored.

Today technology has given a new twist on this process, allowing mechanised industry, creating artificial intelligence, food, and insemination. Such unnatural community structure creates even more isolation and extends solitary confinement where individuals are completely dependent on the system to survive. His life is a status Quo independence only.

Environmentally, there are too many people on Earth, but economics-wise, there are too few to keep the system going.

In developing and Third World countries, communities still have relatively large families. They till the soil and obtain water by Themselves. It is almost as if We'll all soon wake up and realise it's all over before We even start to live Sustainably.

Our history is a history of wars and power struggles where peace is merely an interruption of war. The longest period of peace in history was Pax Romana, given that there were one-third of enslaved people on the Italian Peninsula then, and there was not much left to conquer & civilise. War influences too much of Our culture, even famous literary works such as 'War & Peace,' and 'Iliad & Odyssey.' Today We're bombarded with violent movies, series, & games. Let's focus on Peace now. It is crucial for the survival of Mankind to create a free society while retaining the basic principles for happiness: education, family, health, & sustainability.

We are all familiar with the Ten Commandments:

1. *I am the Lord thy God, Thou shalt have no other gods before me*
2. *Thou shalt not make unto thee any graven image*
3. *Thou shalt not take the name of the Lord thy God in vain*
4. *Remember the sabbath day, to keep it holy*
5. *Honour thy father and thy mother*
6. *Thou shalt not murder*
7. *Thou shalt not commit adultery*
8. *Thou shalt not steal*
9. *Thou shalt not bear false witness against thy neighbour*
10. *Thou shalt not covet*

There is another set of instructions known as Georgia Guidestones:

1. *Maintain humanity under 500,000,000 in perpetual balance with nature.*
2. *Guide reproduction wisely – improving fitness and diversity.*
3. *Unite humanity with a living new language.*
4. *Rule Passion – Faith – Tradition – and all things with tempered reason.*
5. *Protect people and nations with fair laws and just courts.*
6. *Let all nations rule internally resolving external disputes in a world court.*
7. *Avoid petty laws and useless officials.*
8. *Balance personal rights with social duties.*
9. *Prize truth – beauty – love – seeking harmony with the infinite.*
10. *Be not a cancer on the earth – Leave room for nature – Leave room for nature.*

In the words of **Richard Heinberg,** *maybe it's time we all just chill out* and let's reorganise the system in symbiosis with Nature.

So the choice is individually and collectively Yours, Ours! But We've wrongly arranged Our values. We centred Our Civilisation around petty trivialities of the daily grind. We've separated Life from the machine, and We are slaves to this System that We keep running by fearing Life. So, We keep enjoying the false security, the enslaving emotional comfort of Society – Civilisation – the nation of civils.

"It is no measure of health to be well adjusted to a profoundly sick society." **Jiddu Krishnamurti**

Now, how do We fix this mess, my Dear Humans?
We fix it by having the courage to admit to Ourselves that We live a lie, that Our values are upside down, that We're the cowards hiding behind private properties, TV screens, bank accounts, social profiles, a mask of being civilised – the damn Status Quo. We Wake Up from the illusion that We are the pinnacle of evolution and See the most obvious reality: the One Earth, with its basic laws of impermanence & natural cycles!

We See, realise, understand, learn from practice, and Take Action:

Sustainable Action based on Life itself

AI Technology

Given the Scale and Complexity of Our current Civilisation,
which is already entirely dependent on computational technology,
We can only keep developing it to make Our global lives easier.

Only 30 years ago, computers went into global production. That is,
the digital evolution, and We are right in the middle of it. That, in turn,
gives rise to Artificial Intelligence (AI), as it is a natural, technological
progression of computative ability. Soon We'll have robots walking
around, as We already have robotised industries, driverless cars,
self-serving restaurants, and all sorts of tech and robotic gadgets.

But robots will never be Conscious. They can only remain programmed
to perform a better and more precise interaction with the environment,
with the values that serve Us. They will programme themselves, of course,
because they'll do it better than We can, under Our primary instructions.

Now, can this get out of hand? Can We end up in a scenario where robots
take over? Yes, everything is possible, but this can only happen within the
computational complexity of the programmes & algorithms within which
they are operating. Robots will never be able to make Conscious decisions.
They will never have free will or choice. They will never and can't ever be
Self-aware. We can only programme them to the level of perfection that
only gives the appearance of Intelligence or even Consciousness,
depending on the sophistication and speed of the programme.

"AI will be the best or worst thing ever for humanity." Elon Musk

We'll thus be able to programme robots to look and behave as the 'perfect'
Human being, with all the values in their system. They will be infinitely
intelligent, but they will not be Aware. Intelligence is not the measure
of Consciousness. Consciousness is the measure of Consciousness.
How do We measure the level of Consciousness then?
Consciousness is Self-evident, Self-Aware!

If We can replace most Human labour with technology,
We must be sure to have new values in place before that happens.

What does the Human being do when freed from labour? Since most
average people have no hobbies or Life interests other than work and
being at home with their families, how do We motivate Them to interact
with society outside of work? How do We create new meaning?

Responsibility for this falls to the Global community to provide this as
part of Our primary education about Life. Our goal must be to secure a
Sustainable future for all Humans within a healthy environment. So, if
We achieve this through technological and AI progression, We must do
it in correspondence with Our innermost Human values. If We replace
the values that make Us Human, what is the point of securing such a non-
Human future? Can We save Ourselves by turning Ourselves into robots?

> *"Far from being the smartest possible biological species, we are
> probably better thought of as the stupidest possible biological species
> capable of starting a technological civilization."* **Nick Bostrom**

By its natural evolutionary process through Human development,
technological progress will demand We merge with machines.
So as the environment becomes more hostile for healthy biological
Human Life, people will start implanting robotic parts, artificial limbs,
eyes, lungs, hearts, eventually even the brain, giving Them the
illusion of Consciousness. But that will be the final conscious act,
for They will commit biological, and thus Consciousness, suicide.

Moreover, the reason They'll certainly do this is that Their AI replicas
will look & behave exactly as They do, and even to any desired perfection.
The transition to these digital & mechanical improvements & necessities
will happen naturally, and this is indeed already happening. There are
a billion people working on computers as Their job or involved with
programs & machinery. And We have a majority of the population
dependent on personal mobile phones & devices. It's becoming impossible
to function in modern society without involving Yourself with technology.

The younger generations especially are becoming obsessed with looks & body improvements, such as silicone, implants, and even gender change. They are largely influencing Our industry & economy in this direction of losing Our biological nature and shifting Our collective mentality.

People who are not interested in this will die off and will be replaced by Those transitioning. This understanding is as simple as an evolutionary process. We cannot stop this process, but We could learn to differentiate Our biological and Conscious decisions from those purely mental desires or even existential needs for technology.

If We can replace most of the Human body with artificial limbs & implants, it is advisable to first know what it means to be a Human and how far We want to go down that artificial path. If We can create perfect robots, what will stop Us from replacing all Humans with robots, justifying this by making sure that Civilisation survives or becomes ideal in every moral, environmental, and Cosmic sense?

So are We going to turn Ourselves into robots without even living as a True, genuine Human Civilisation? I would love to Live as a Human Being first before deciding to go down the AI road entirely.

In many ways, We already live like robots, emotionless and with no sense of responsibility for the Global community. We are primarily slaves to satisfying Our egos. The fact that We already live in such a complex technological Civilisation, while some basic Life needs are still not being secured for All Humans, is a sign that We're even now failing to determine Our Humanity, Our moral values, and Our necessities. And this doesn't give any hopeful prediction about how AI evolution will go.

> *"The development of full artificial intelligence could spell the end of the human race...It would take off on its own, and re-design itself at an ever increasing rate. Humans, who are limited by slow biological evolution, couldn't compete, and would be superseded."* **Stephen Hawking**

But if We can't function in peace without AI, then it is more frightening

not to create it than to create it, for, without it, We'll not survive.
And of course, as We examined, it's a game of rolling the dice,
Conscious decisions & chances that will remain even with AI.

It's not a question of whether We need new technologies, for We do need
them, but do We understand the implications of AI technology sufficiently
enough to be safe & sure in how to manage it, with certainty in survival?

We need and We must use any new Technology, especially Artificial
Intelligence, but We must use it Intelligently & Sustainably!

In order to best deal with these existential & moral questions, We
must first become Humans to determine what serves Our Humanity,
what makes Us more of who We are, and who We want to be.

How can We be sure that We're not already robots Ourselves, or
that We don't live in a Simulation which gives Us this sense of real Life,
where all We know is the perception of the World, not the World itself?
The Answer is that We don't know the ultimate structure of The World or
the Universe, and We can't know what sort of reality We're experiencing.

Even if We are in the simulation and only Our Conscious experience is real,
while all else is the simulated projection, We can only speculate on the type
of reality that lies behind such a simulation. It can be anything imaginable,
any multi-dimensional kind of existence, where the
Universe as such doesn't even exist, nor even do biological Beings.

Our particular simulation could be as unique as any other simulation,
which would give credence to the simulation argument and justify the
need to run an infinite number of them. Whoever would start such
simulated realities would also allow the evolution of artificial intelligence
to unfold within itself, where simulated Universes recognise themselves
in Consciousness. They would, in turn, run Their simulations because
They'll arrive at the same need, to keep simulations going indefinitely,
for that's the only way the evolutionary fractal structure of

Conscious Beings can continue. If there is indeed one original simulation in place, it would mean that all other simulations directly depend on the first one – a continuing pyramid scheme.

These options take Us to the infinity scenario, the eternal division of existential phenomena. It would mean that Life is a never-ending self-perpetuating and self-replicating maze of simulations, where the only thing We can be sure of is Our Self-awareness.

That would also mean that, with today's Scientific investigations, We're merely observing the illusory reality of the simulation. Probing it in detail and getting to the end of possibilities with fundamental particles.

So imagine if You're wearing simulation glasses, and You want to find out what such a reality is made of. You could only discover an illusory field of pixels, the holographic bits of information, and You could never leave the simulation. It could be terminated only by the outside source.

So again, the only thing left for Us to hold on to is the very knowing of whatever experience might be perceived. We can only ever be certain that We are Conscious. But can Consciousness itself be simulated, or resume the type of conduits, such as the Soul, the Human body, or the computer, as a window into the apparent reality, regardless of whether its an original or simulated one?

> *"The problem is that the presence of intelligence does not imply the presence of consciousness: whereas a computer may effectively emulate the information processing that occurs in a human brain, this does not mean that the calculations performed by the computer will be accompanied by private inner experience."* **Bernardo Kastrup**

Only Consciousness Knows that it is Conscious; no Human, robot, animal, plant, planet, sun, galaxy, or Universe is Conscious. They are what is being perceived in Consciousness.

Nothing can be Conscious by itself! Only Consciousness is Conscious

Diet

We Are Eating Ourselves to Extinction!

Right Now, the Population is obsessed with taste buds
and addictive cravings. To STOP and Reverse this Unhealthy,
Environment Polluting & Destroying Behaviour is one of the Great
Challenges We need to point out to Inform & Educate the Masses.

I would love if People cut down on meat consumption to once or twice
per week. Rather than basing Their Diet so heavily on meat, They would
get only those needed essentials from a minimally destructive amount.

People should base Their Diet on Watery produce such as Vegetables
& Fruits – half thermally processed and half Raw. Then there are many
options with Potatoes, Rice, all the Grain Cereals, Seeds, and Legumes.

This type of Diet would reduce Global meat production by up to 70%.
As most agriculture is food for farm animals, We would thus save some
50% of arable land, which could be Re-planted in the form of Forests
& Vegetation, Crucially Increasing Levels of Oxygen and Collective
Green Consciousness of The Worlds Population for Generations!

Furthermore, the remainder of what the meat production is left
should be as Organic & Natural as possible, to ensure We produce
only the best, top-quality meat, also preventing any potential
industrial-scale meat production-related deficiencies & diseases.

We Need To Protect Our Waters, Forests, Oceans, Ban Plastic,
Replace Fossil Fuels, and Use Recyclable Materials only!

Transformation STARTS with YOU & Me!
We Don't Need To Fight Anyone,
We Just Need To Buy More Economically, and
Industry Will Adapt & Produce Accordingly

Environment

The Greatest Issue We face Today is
the Sheer Lack of Environmental Awareness!

We are indoctrinated into the illusion of a materialistic
ever-expanding economy! But We can't survive indefinitely
without Healthy Food, Clean Water, Fresh Air & Soil.

This means that Our failure to connect to Nature and realise
its crucial Value for Human as well as every Other Life on Earth is
not a subject of personal opinion, but it's the very Nature of Life!

*"The truth is: the natural world is changing. And we are totally dependent
on that world. It provides our food, water and air. It is the most precious
thing we have and we need to defend it."* **Sir David Attenborough**

Earth gives Us Everything for Free, and Everything We
use to live comes from Nature. Yet, Humanity is living
blindfolded in the face of this most apparent correlation in Life.

If We care more for possessions than the very Earth which allows
this Life to happen, then We have an obvious & fundamental flaw
of mis-prioritised moral and Life values, being ego-obsessed, which
proves Our complete disconnection from the Reality around Us, failing
to comprehend the importance of Our Individual Impact in The World.

Natural Earth is Our First, Primal & Foremost Relative, Family, & Home!

If Civilisation ends in Catastrophe, it would be self-evident how
wrongly We have set up Our Existential priorities. But it doesn't have
to end to prove this. The Reality has been evident for a long time
already. And it will get worse before it gets better. That is the
natural progress of societies. They Rise & Fall, and We are
reaching the point of breaking, both Nature and the System.

We've been disconnected from Nature and Our True Selves for millennia!
Humans have been hypnotised & robbed of Their Soul Essence, Their
very Being. We care more about the glory of an imaginary God,
or a Lifetime of hedonism & fun, rather than the Earth
which We completely depend upon!
This type of behaviour is just an excuse for throwing Our hands in the
air and taking no responsibility for the actual Real World We inhabit –
the Natural World of animals, raw materials, and resources.

How much longer do We need to isolate Ourselves to understand
that the World We've created is useless in the long-term?
Nothing We've ever done will matter if We're unable to Continue
Life in Freedom & Sustainability for Generations to Come.

We don't need an infinite growth of the economy for the
World to function normally. We need to Start functioning
normally for The World to Live Sustainably!

We need The New Social & Economic Order,
We need The New World Order, In Effect!

We need to Stop Constructing and Start Reorganising Our Living Space!
We need to Re-educate the Masses, Inform & Retrain Ourselves Wisely!

How do We construct a sustainable, healthy environment?
Our Cities shouldn't be larger than 1 million inhabitants. The size of
the city needs to be accompanied by the same size of parks & recreational
areas, in addition to the National Park that's in proximity, which should
equate to being at least five times larger than the entire city.

With the localised economy, this type of permacultural,
ecosystemic city design will allow for more connectivity
with Nature, and in general, Better Life & Air Quality.

Demand This Transformation and Be the Change!
Firstly Environmental, then Sociological

<u>Documentary</u>

Life on Earth is not a Movie. It is The Documentary!

You do Understand that more & more Life on Earth will
never be the same again. That All areas of Health and
Sustainability are decreasing dramatically every year.

Clean Water, Air, and Soil should be Our ONLY Concern!
These are the Essential Elements of Life. You can
manage without anything else except these 3!

We can call them NATURE, in General.

And We're playing Russian roulette with Nature.
We are hitting each other hard.
We're chopping up parts of Nature, which
backfires on Us in the form of catastrophes,
as lack of a healthy environment,
and as bad living conditions.
So in truth, We are knocking Ourselves out!
We are hitting Our heads against the wall by Our own doing.

Let Us take an example of this on a smaller scale!
Imagine You live in the closed space of Your house & backyard.
Here You have a place to be and an entire garden of vegetation.
You also have a stream & trees there. You have everything You
need to survive indefinitely if You keep such symbiosis going.

Now, what would happen if You cut down some trees and
built another house because You need to accommodate Your
growing family, and You also need more space to grow more food,
so You cut down even more trees to make space for new arable land?
You now have a lack of air for a start, so this experiment
would come to an abrupt End quickly.

But now, consider tribal people!
They would never cross that line where Their communal self-interest
would wreak havoc on the environment. They keep Their numbers
in check without disturbing the delicate balance.
They have only a certain number of newcomers,
depending on what Nature can accommodate.

This, which We've been doing for so long, is remaining 100% ignorant
towards all these natural laws. We're spreading uncontrollably and
depleting the oxygen, borrowing Our time from future generations.
We are throwing everything into this one century. We're having incredible
global fun – *The Great Burning* – without thinking that We need to Wake
Up in the morning and go to work. We live oblivious to the essential
symbiosis of Nature. We are teenagers having a party, having no real
view or comprehension of The World. We're playing a planetary
monopoly game, with Our heads in the illusion of success clouds.

Definition of a Virus:
An infectious agent, too small to be seen on the host,
thus having a harmful or corrupting influence, capable of
copying itself and typically has a detrimental effect, such as
creating a system that destroys its host and its environment.

Sadly again, just like Human behaviour on Earth!

All the mess in The World has one basic cause: unconsciousness,
non-intelligence, which in practical terms means the abuse of
power, manipulation, and poverty, leading to overpopulation.

150 million people are born each year, and many of Them
end up abandoned since most of Them are not planned,
for which reason there are 50 million abortions yearly.

It would be the moral thing to first adopt & educate Those abandoned
children before making new Ones! And instead of breeding & feeding
billions of home pets, can't We feed these children who are left starving?

A permanent solution is to Educate All the People in the first place.

"Give a bowl of rice to a man and you will feed him for a day. Teach him how to grow his own rice and you will save his life." **Confucius**

We mostly use freedom to satisfy Our unconscious selfish non-moral egoistic ways. We can't agree to organise, educate, and share this World in peace. Instead, We go to War and suffer because of Our bigotry.

"Too often we participate in the globalization of indifference. May we strive instead to live global solidarity." **Pope Francis**

If We stop fighting about Our egos and divert the World's resources to issues that actually matter, We can free Ourselves from this slavery to the system and start working for the benefit of All.

"Take all that money we spend on weapons and defenses each year and instead spend it feeding and clothing and educating the poor of the world, which it would pay for many times over, not one human being excluded, and we could explore space, together, both inner and outer, forever, in peace." **Bill Hicks**

The suppressed technology of unlimited free-producing energy devices, such as magnetic rotors, is the way in which to solve energy issues!

But even if We were to have all the clean, free energy available, without the need to use fossil fuels, We would still be facing the growing Social crisis, food quality degradation, and lack of a living habitat.

It is clear that Dramatic Changes in All areas of Life are needed! We can't afford a growing population and expect a high living standard.

We need to STOP all construction works, all unnecessary buying & spending, and NOW, We should implement the Greatest Environmental Conservation in History:

REPLANTING THE LOST HALF OF THE WORLD'S FORESTS

What Can We Do

It is the Greatest question always deluding Our Society:
Where will Humanity go from this point? The answer is as simple
as how Conscious Our every intention is, how fundamentally
Symbiosed it is with the Ecosystem and how Sustainable it is.

Corporate powers lead this World through a monetary system
that is based on infinite growth, which is impossible on a finite
planet. But if You try to change the Status Quo, You'll be
swept away by the powers of the United Corporations
that collectively masquerade as a Democracy.

> *There is a war on for your mind!* **INFO**
> Alex Jones   *WARS*

The very fact that money exists means the system is corrupted and
open for abuse. If We organised Ourselves, We wouldn't need money.
The bigger the system, the more control it needs, a lot like God.

We all fear doing what We really want. Facing those fears is the
measure of happiness. And it is not about money or possessions,
but about being Yourself, even if that means going broke or being
left alone, but We must stay true to Ourselves. We have to
be Our True Selves to be in real Joy!

As long as Your TV is on, as long as the mass Status Quo hypnosis is
influencing Your basic views of The World, You're not going to start
thinking for Yourself, and eventually, with enough mercy & grace,
break through that compulsive mind-habit, which is something all
foolosophers have failed to see as the liberating insight indeed.

*Until We Awaken Our Freedoms of expressing Ourselves as Unique
Beings, and Come Together from that Greater Will to See Every Other
Need & Right to Live Met, We're not going to see a Large-scale Awakening!*

Ask Yourself: is My Life Helping The World to be a Better Place, at least through Sustainable Engagement in My Local Community? That starts with Education and the Intelligent Organisation of Earth's resources. We can't just have the perfect environment and living conditions handed to us on a plate, as We'll keep abusing it. Instead of waiting for Our elected officials, We need to create so-called Utopia by Ourselves, from Our understanding, as this is the only way We will take care of it!

What We Can Do:
Take Responsibility For Your Own Actions!
Be the Living Embodiment and Practical example of the
type of Life needed for this Change in Awareness to Happen!

"If you want the best the World has to offer, offer the World your best."
Neal Donald Walsch

When We Comprehend the Enormity of the Situation,
We see Humanity and The Earth as THE WORLD!
There are not 8 billion Lives on the Planet, the fact is,
there is only ONE LIFE and it's called The Earth!

*"A new consciousness is developing which sees the earth
as a single organism and recognizes that an organism at
war with itself is doomed. We are one planet."* **Carl Sagan**

It is already a miracle that these 8 billion People have
been functioning together without a major war for decades.
And Now, are We going to fight a New World War History,
or Create The New History of THE WORLD

*   *   *

STOP! RELAX! Feel Your HEART and Put That Into ACTION!
LIFE IS That SIMPLE

Crossroads

We Now stand at the Crossroads
of Our Civilisation's Destiny.

The Earth is in Peril, Dear Humans!
It Needs Your Help, and Most Urgently So!

This is the most urgent Message, for the most uncertain times!

I ask You to look around You and tell me what You see.
What do You see in Your proximity compared to the World at large?

Can You not See the lies that have been pulled over Our eyes,
blinding Us to the truth. The Truth of Our Own demise!

We are in such a Complex Network on Earth, that nobody knows
what will happen next. Until mass Consciousness is still on the
let go, the World will be ruled by unconscious yearnings.

It has now been long in the making, Infinitely long to be precise!
And doesn't that make You shiver, doesn't it make You proud?

There is an Infinity behind Us, fellow Humans,
and Eternity ahead of Us!

All that ever Was, IS, and Ever Will Be,
is happening right Now, in this very moment,
With You, as the Centre Point of the Mystery.

Without You, there is no Past, Present, or Future.
With You, there is All Presence in Present.

The past was Yesterday's Today, and
the Future will be Tomorrow's Today.

If You do All right, Right Now, there won't be
a past to dwell upon nor a future to be afraid of.
There is only Today's feast of the Now fruits!

As Mother Teresa so clearly put it:
"We fear the future because We are wasting today."

We must Stop wasting Today's Opportunities.
We must Stop missing the Present Possibilities and
Start bravely creating Our Promised Futures, Today!

Stop chasing the cut and Start cutting the chase!
These are critical times to Unite Our Earthly family under
the Same Colour of Consciousness, to speed up the Transformation
and make Life collectively more enjoyable & sustainable for All.

Let's Start Healing the Earth, for the Earth
and Our species are Counting on Us!
We must Start Counting on Them too,
and We must do it NOW

*   *   *

*In the coming decade,
the Greatest Priority Must Be to Secure
Basic Necessities of Life for All Humans,
to Eradicate Poverty!*

*The Foundation of a Society which tolerates
and ignores This Freedom to Live
is a Crime against Humanity,
it is a Crime against Itself!*

Life is the Right of Everyone

<u>Life</u>

How precious Life on Earth is! How Delicate & Alive!

"Thriving is the natural flow of life.
If nature teaches us anything, it is that life is meant to work
and that like every living thing, our purpose is to thrive." THRIVE

Life on Earth is the Most Magnificent Imaginary Existence
Ever to have appeared in the Consciousness' Universe!
How do I Know This?
Because You Are Here!

You are here as that Divine Presence.
You are here in the most original & pristine form
ever imaginable for Existence to dream of! Although
this fact is temporarily obscured by the unconscious mind.

How now do We transcend the limited self to protect &
preserve this fascination of Living Beings on Earth?

We must get Our thoughts straight!
We must let go of Our egos' attachment to things.
We must sustain this intimate freedom to be As We Are.
One with the Universal scale of small things,
coherently vibrating in the GREATER scheme.

Hear me Now, Fellow Humans. Listen to my innermost calling
to reawaken Your sleeping beast in the form of Love & Beauty.
Have We not suffered enough? Have We not Killed God
enough, as Nietzsche *famously proclaimed?*

This Must Stop, for Your & Our collective Wellbeing
depend on it, both Now and in the Future, thus for
Our Children and Our Children's Children!

We should engage all of Humanity to work on sustainability and endeavour to use all of Earth's resources to invest in Scientific breakthroughs. That, in turn, can free Us from manual labour and secure the healthy technological progress of Our Civilisation and thus forever be assured of Our place amongst the Stars!

Instead, We waste most of the resources on single-use fun, financing endless entertainment industries, engaging in wasteful, destructive wars, and destroying precious materials, rare substances, and minerals for the sake of pleasuring Our egos.

You know deep down within Yourself that the Crisis is Here, that it is Real, and that this Fight for Survival will eventually Happen. You have Felt it for so long now. We have All felt it for decades!

We Are the Canvas upon which Our Destiny is being Determined & Set Upon, We Are the Sole Fate upon which Our Children's Future will be Foreseen & Sealed. We Are the Ones We've been Waiting for all Along. So Perform Your Part Well Dear Human, Or There Will Be No Theatre Left To Play.

But We will stand United again, as We always did, as We previously stood together in arms, against all odds, with a wall against Our back. In this knowing that there is no turning back, We have fought like We never did before. We have stood, brave & strong, against tyranny, We have stood fast against oppression & slavery, We Have Won Our Freedom, again, anew, and Again!

It is an Honour to fight alongside You once again!

It is Our Planetary & Universal impulse calling Us Home, to raise the banners of Human Dignity and Soul Power, for We'll Never Give Up on the Life We Own & Are!

"We Will Never Surrender, No Matter The Cost"

Handshake

We All share this One Earth, and most People struggle to survive.

Remember Them All: family, friends, relatives, People of all Nations!

Remember Everyone who ever Lived & Died,
alongside All today's Human Souls.

There are almost 8 billion People on Earth Now!
If You wanted to Shake Hands with every person for
just One Second, it would take 250 years to do so!

We are All Seeds of the same Life!
We are All Children of the same Universe!
We are All Love, which is the Life of God!

You don't know this by the something We all have which is different,
like body & mind, but by the something We all have in common,
which is the capacity to be Self Aware, to Know Your Being!

*"I am convinced that the way forward for the human race is to recognize
and protect the fundamental right of sovereignty over consciousness, to
help the human spirit to grow rather than to wither, and to nurture our
innate capacity for love and mutual respect. The old ways are broken and
bankrupt and new ways are struggling to be born. Each one of us with our
own talents, and by our own choices, has a part to play in that process."*
Graham Hancock

The more Consciousness You invite into Your daily tasks,
the more Awareness You'll Awaken into Your moments' Life.
You'll see the World with more reason, understanding, compassion,
fascination, appreciation, Self-reflection, and Love!

So Live it,
Be It

A <u>New World</u>

Good & bad are inadequate measures of morality, for what is considered to be good in one culture may be seen as immoral in another. We must measure global character in terms of Human condition, necessity, and sustainability. In other words, it is a question of adaptability, so there can't be fixed laws about what is good/wrong or moral/immoral.

Suppose in a catastrophic situation, the survival of Mankind depended solely on skilled individuals. In that case, We should give shelter & food to those who are the best at adapting for survival, who contribute the most. Those are the scientists who can most easily salvage what is left of Our technology & resources and put it to further use the quickest. Then comes everyone else by looking at particular necessities of the situation. Because We can't have fixed laws on morality, Humanity has developed entire spheres of reasonings; philosophy, justice, politics, theology, etc.

To, in a way, jumpstart that debate is to focus on the current situation of the practical benefits. For exp., meat production & consumption is taken for granted in most of the World, and it is also regarded as immoral in many cultures. Looking at this from a purely environmental perspective, it's not sustainable, and it is with other pollutions the greatest issue today.

You can argue the morality of eating meat, but You can't argue the environmental consequences of such action. The bottom line of this truth is asking: does the action benefit sustainable Life? Does it bring about general wellbeing and is that wellbeing rooted in sustainability? We must make decisions based not on morality but Sustainability.

Sustainability again is an entirely new science itself, and it can't be put into laws either. It depends on the current level of progress, so it is entirely based on science. In order to create sustainable technology, We must first use fossil fuels and invest all Our efforts into researching, developing, testing, and applying those new technologies. It is a risky investment into the future, but it can't be done any other way.

We can't jump ahead of evolution, but We can inform and educate
the Population to allocate more resources to Science & Sustainability.

So, what type of World should We Envision?

I See a borderless World! Where Our National Pride
is merely symbolic in meaning, a ceremonial gesture of
Acknowledging Our Historical & Cultural Circumstances
as Flavours of Authentic Regional Diversity and products
of Unique Climate, language, art, ideas, and designs.

I want a World where You have One ID Card for everything,
and You can travel anywhere in the World without restrictions.
There should be no obstacles to Human Movement.
Otherwise, it is Not Freedom!

Such a World is based on long-term Sustainability, and this
means No non-recyclable products. No more single-use items,
No more garbage! That also means No domesticated animals,
meat production, possessions & isolations, no army, police, or jobs.

You Socialise and Contribute as a Community, Freely & Always.

*"As long as there are prisons, police, armies, navies; we are not
civilized. When the Earth joins together and uses the Earth intelligently,
that will be the beginning of civilization."* **Jacque Fresco**

With no money, Your values will shift to Real Life Values!
Ones felt and always experienced, for they're not separate from
how You live and interact. Every Person and every Tree is You!

It is a World where the First thing Children learn at School is
to Plant a Tree! And Trees will be Everywhere, Plants, Bushes,
Grass, Flowers. Every Surface that was taken from Nature
Will Be Restored & Covered With Nature Again!

In such a World, People don't sit in front of a television, but in Back & Front Gardens, Living in the Moment, Witnessing the Amazing Growth of Vegetation, Organic Fruits & Vegetables.

There would be mostly see-through walls allowing for the most natural Light to enter, similar to how We construct modern office buildings so that everybody is aware of each Other constantly and nobody feels isolated or private. This would compel You to present Your Best Self always, which would become Your only Self by giving You no other alternatives. You would be able to See everything and what Everyone around You is doing. You would always be fully connected to Your immediate surroundings, and You'd be able to move in all directions. This type of Universal, basic, natural freedom will create a Utopian Society within a few Generations.

You will be an Ancient & Wise Human Being,
Integrating Modern Technological Society!

In every way, it is the Green *Venus Project!*

"The intelligent use of science and technology are the tools with which to achieve a new direction." **Jacque Fresco**

The Only and the Best way Humanity can Preserve
its Soul, its Earthly Bond, and its Destiny
to Explore the Stars,
In Peace

*   *   *

Humanity is a species dependent on the Sun.
It Gives Us Life, and We use it
in many ways & forms.
That's what We Are, Reshapers of Energy

Utopia

I see a Wonderful Future! Our Industry is adapting to environmental, sociological, cultural, spiritual, and other Planetary challenges. It's recalibrating its machinery to power Us into The New Age of Human Achievements – The Rise of Mega Machines! Imagine enormous dome polyglass palaces. A Sustainable World with mechanised, computerised structures the size of cities, huge as far as the eyes can see, stretching from horizon to horizon, and functioning entirely on clean energy. They sit in the most unlikely of places, where We thought We could not build. But now, these places enable Us to produce food, energy & materials. They are isolated from the outside influences and have their own atmosphere. So We can continue growing the freshest, most organic, tastiest, cleanest, eco-friendliest produce, with Zero pollution. Vast benefits with No negative consequences for the Environment! There are no People inside there as We can't allow any biological interference. The Entire Project is fully Quantum Computerised, Mechanised, & Sealed from any contaminants. We deliver all this Goodness to Our cities instantly via tunnel tubes. That is what We agreed to, that is what We needed to do! In Our Cities, We don't have as much visible technology anymore. We tried, but it was not serving Our Enlightened Expansion. So We covered it up. We put the Machines far into the landscape, away from Our vision, away from Our thoughts, away from Our Children. Now We Live in Sustainable Peace! We Live At One with Technology but are completely free of It. In this way, We keep All of Nature Pristine & Authentic, allowing Evolution to Continue Naturally.
We Live in Utopian Cities integrated into Nature!
And Our Industry, Our Machinery, is Isolated from both. This is the Holy Trinity and the Promised Garden of Eden! That is Our Hope, Our Secret, Our Heaven! That is Our Future, Our Present, Our HOME

*   *   *

The Earth is a Beautiful System, a Natural Tapestry,
allowing the development of this Human Dream

The Unity

*"The day science begins to study non-physical phenomena,
it will make more progress in one decade than in all the
previous centuries of its existence."* **Nikola Tesla**

If We line up the Universal Scale of Things,
We start as subatomic particles, bits of
information, atoms, elements, molecules, and Life.

This Life has evolved as the Natural World of vegetation,
animals, Humans, or in the broader sense, as planets, stars,
galaxies, and the Universe, with 96% more things going
on than We can see, observe, measure, or comprehend.

All these experiences are happening in Consciousness, where
the matter is in the densest form that Consciousness can take.
And even this solid, dense matter itself is becoming denser and
so compacted that it seems to disappear within itself, which
We, at least mathematically, observe them as Black holes.

Modern Science still holds that matter exists on its own,
and Consciousness is a by-product of biological complexity,
that is, of the neural intricacy of Our brains' activities.

That is where We need to go back to Our experience and
trace it down to Consciousness. Thus We notice how matter
and the brain exist as an experience within Consciousness, and
rather than reacting and giving rise to experiences, instead,
they arise as a multitude of vibrational variables, as simple
facts of observation, as the knower of experiencing.

*"Deep down the consciousness of mankind is one. This is a virtual
certainty because even in the vacuum matter is one; and if we don't
see this, it's because we are blinding ourselves to it."* **David Bohm**

The Universe is a type of collective solid dream, in the sense that We do experience persistent and localised sense perceptions through it. But it is merely the most common experience of the mind which creates this tunnel of time & space We call the Universe, and Consciousness is All this at Once. It is not everywhere, rather, everything is in IT!

This One Consciousness which gives rise to all objective reality, appears to Us as individual experience and therefore provides Us with the sense of Ourselves. But as soon as We lose this material sense of separateness when Our body dies, We experience a transcendental Wholeness again, The Unity, which is the Beingness.

We can, however, *Die before We Die* and experience this freedom from localised perception and Our minds even Now. That is increasingly becoming the only necessity if Our Civilisation wants to survive the challenges ahead.   *"Evolve or die"* **Eckhart Tolle**

By definition of Conscious Evolution, We'll witness the melting of Our rigid beliefs and transformation of Religion into Spirituality, Politics into Livelihood, System into Sustainability. We will also, by definition of Progress in Science, witness Unification of General Relativity with Quantum Mechanics, Cosmology with Quanta, of BIG with small within One Theory of Everything describing the Universe.

This need for Unification of All Life requires Us to Unite Science and Consciousness, or, in other words, ***CONSCIOUSNESS & The WORLD !***

"The two can, and I believe eventually will, be reunited. Their meeting point is consciousness. When science sees consciousness to be a fundamental quality of reality, and religion takes God to be the light of consciousness shining within us all, the two worldviews start to converge." **Peter Russell**

Only when We See, Feel, and Know Ourselves as One World, One Nation, One Race, shall We Act as One Consciousness

Service to Humanity

It's not about You. It's about Serving!
Serving the People around You, the Community,
the Planet, Serving All the Life on Earth!

Let go of the need to satisfy Your ego, experience the benefits
of dedicating Your efforts to Others, to collective healing and mutual
growth. There is an Increasing Strength when One's motivation comes
from the Soul power by working on the Livelihood of All. This Light
Unites Humanity in its Spiritual Origin, Fire, and Destiny.

*Privatisation and isolation leads to separation, but it is
a Heartfelt Communication that Betters Generations!*

You will forgive my weaknesses and be kind to my strength.
Everything negative is not who You are but a lack of education.
And how can We blame anyone for being uneducated instead of
Ourselves for not being conscious enough to see the light of this truth?
We can only ever inspire & educate. To help rather than blame.
*This Spark of Freedom to better Ourselves Together
defines the definition of Teamwork.*

Ask Anyone: How can I help You?
Ask Yourself: How can I help myself by Serving Others?

*"Life's most persistent and urgent question is, 'What are
you doing for others?'"* **Martin Luther King Jr.**

In the Depth of Your Being, and
Knowing Their Happiness Is Your Joy,
Their Prosperity Is Your Wellbeing,
Their Future Is Your Peace,
Their Love Is Your Light,
We Ascend in Our Consciousness

Consciousness in The World

What is the main goal in Life?
What would be the real purpose of a Civilisation?
It is to Survive by Thriving!

How do We create such a prosperous environment and preserve Our
Human Heritage, Love, & Wisdom? We need to connect, that is, Awaken
to Our natural roots and Consciousness. Human Beings need education
that is not based on belief or fear but on the very foundation of Life.

*"Reason, decency, tolerance, empathy and hope are human traits that we should aspire
to, not because we seek reward of eternal life or because we fear the punishment of
a supernatural being, but because they define our humanity."* Jim Al-Khalili

No new or old ideologies can ever withstand Our constant ever-present
Spiritual reality, out of which this material world appears. When You
stop doing everything that is not inherent and needed to thrive, only
eternal presence remains. Going back 5,000 years, We already have
astonishing scriptures of such realisations in ancient text, which
describes that primordial Oneness with clear and poetic beauty.
Realising One's True nature goes hand in hand with Humanity.

As One investigates His true nature, and thus the nature of reality,
He will find Life/Existence to be meaningless. This realisation is the
cornerstone to freedom, through that self-recognition of Consciousness.
This gives Him an awesome responsibility of creating His meanings,
of ascribing purpose to Life. The meaning of Life is to give Life a
meaning/purpose. The base meaning is happiness, which is also
the true Human nature and the two are inseparable: they are One.
Happiness – Community – Wellbeing – Thriving – Awakening

Awakening is Our true birthright. That is why We exist,
to fully integrate
CONSCIOUSNESS into The WORLD

Global Awakening

An interest in the Fundamental Nature of Reality – Consciousness itself – within which the entire Universe, mind and matter appear, implies realising Your True nature, and vice versa. That means seeing how thoughts & feelings are not Our traits, as they arise by themselves, and We're aware of them. Within that free space, We Alone Are Responsible For Our World & Peace!

I Focus and Send Prayers, Blessings, and Healing for the Transformative Progress of Our Civilisation!

We Are Witnessing the Global Awakening of Collective Human Consciousness!

People are choosing Healthier Lifestyles! They are thinking for Themselves, which makes Them more Aware of the World, more Caring, more Spiritual, and more Intelligent.

Their eyes are opening, Their minds expanding to the fact that the only Real issue We face is Environmental Sustainability, and with that, all other differences are proving irrelevant.

"The fact is that no species has ever had such wholesale control over everything on earth, living or dead, as we now have. That lays upon us, whether we like it or not, an awesome responsibility. In our hands now lies not only our own future, but that of all other living creatures with whom we share the earth" Sir David Attenborough

We are now at the Centre of the Life Phenomenon! And it is because of Our Universal Transcendental Values that We can Save Humanity, through that Higher Power by staying Vigilant, Observant, and Humbly Participating in Blessing, Thanking, and Healing! Envision the type of World You want to Live In and what sort of World We want to leave to Our Children.

That Process Takes Place on the Individual Level.
The Global Transformation is the Reflection
of an Inner Awakening!

That Starts with a Conversation!
Talk to Your Families & Friends about this!
Every moment is Important & Crucial in Raising
enough Voices to put Meaningful Practice into Action!

"THE REVOLUTION IS NOW" ZEITGEIST

If You are not demanding and taking responsibility for Your
local & regional Ecosystem, nobody in power will do it either.

There is No Separation between Us & Nature, so there
can't be a separation between People & Governance either!

"The world doesn't belong to leaders. The world belongs to all humanity."
14th Dalai Lama

That is as Crucial an Existential Truth as any should Be.
And it Starts with YOU having the Courage to Act upon It NOW!

"The best time to plant a tree was 20 years ago. The second best time is now."

*   *   *

What We Need Is:

***THE GREEN REVOLUTION
ON A GLOBAL SCALE !***

And We Need It

NOW

<u>Transformation</u>

We have to Work Hard to Revitalise Ourselves!

*Let's Transform Our Neighbourhoods into Natural Oases and Influence
the World's Transformation into a Sustainable, Healthy Environment!*

*Where Every corner of Living Space will Be a Botanical Garden, and
All of Humanity will Be Proud to Live on This Beautiful Earth!*

To Live That Original, Pure, Innocent, Pristine, Natural Way
Is The Highest Excitement! That is Our Dream, that is Our
Vision and the Purpose We Share In on this Planet.
Nothing else will make Us as truly Happy than
Living while Fulfilling Our Maximum Potential.

Seeing Raw Reality and Taking Action are the
only things that matter in the long run!

*"Actions speak louder than words; let your
words teach and your actions speak."* **St. Anthony**

There is a lot of work that We have to do, Personally & Globally.
We Create Our Destiny, so let's Organise it Wisely!

Let's Usher in, Together, the Green Age of Conservation !

Let's make this Sustainable Future Our Present !

In both Our

CONSCIOUSNESS
& The WORLD

To YOU

To LIFE

Thank You

Thank You

Thank You

About the Author

Petar Umiljanović,

was born in Croatia on the 28th of June 1987.

From an early age, He felt strangely connected to and interested in the Universe, Nature, Religion, and Mysteries, along with Science, History, Ufology, Sport, and Music.

Later, profound insights into Psychology, Philosophy, and Spirituality led Him to investigate the True nature of the Self, revealing Consciousness as the only constant Presence.

Upon moving to Ireland and travelling Europe, thus engaging in many arts and activities, especially experiencing a deep relationship with Nature, this book was gradually inspired!

Contact:
petarumiljanovic@gmail.com

SECRET GARDEN

of

INSPIRATION

IMAGINE A SUSTAINABLE PLANET

DESIGN YOUR WELLBEING

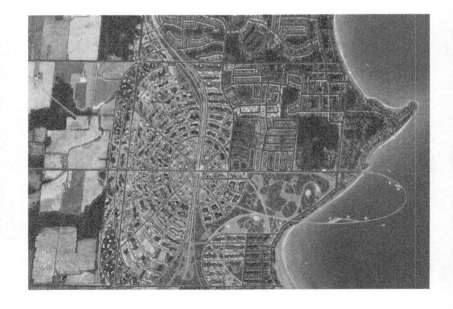

CREATE A GREEN FUTURE TODAY

NOTES

NOTES

Printed in Great Britain
by Amazon